RO176466851

The Simple Joys of Quilting

30 TIMELESS QUILT PROJECTS

✳

Joan Hanson and Mary Hickey

Martingale™
& COMPANY

Credits

President . . . . Nancy J. Martin
CEO . . . . Daniel J. Martin
Publisher . . . . Jane Hamada
Editorial Director . . . . Mary V. Green
Managing Editor . . . . Tina Cook
Technical Editor . . . . Ursula Reikes
Copy Editor . . . . Liz McGehee
Design and Production Manager. . Stan Green
Illustrator . . . . Robin Strobel
Text Designer . . . . Trina Stahl
Cover Designer . . . . Stan Green
Photographer . . . . Brent Kane

That Patchwork Place® is an imprint of
Martingale & Company™.

The Simple Joys of Quilting:
30 Timeless Quilt Projects
©2001 by Joan Hanson and Mary Hickey

Martingale & Company
20205 144th Ave. NE
Woodinville, WA 98072-8478 USA
www.martingale-pub.com

Printed in China
05 04 03 02 01   6 5 4 3 2 1

**Library of Congress Cataloging-in-
Publication Data**

Hanson, Joan.
    The simple joys of quilting: 30 timeless
quilt projects/Joan Hanson and Mary Hickey.
       p. cm.
    ISBN 1-56477-383-3
    1. Patchwork—Patterns. 2. Quilting. 3.
Patchwork quilts. I. Hickey, Mary.
II. Title.
TT835 .H4543 2001
746.46'041—dc21   2001034243

Contents

ON THE COVER: Featured quilts are "North Wind" (on the bed), "Friendship Stars" (in the foreground), and "Kristen's Four Patch" (on the wall). The cover was photographed at Pennsylvania Woodworks, Woodinville, Washington.

Preface

WE FEEL SO fortunate to be able to call quiltmaking—designing, creating, teaching, and writing—our job. What a blessing! At the heart of being a woman is the drive to nurture and shelter those around us. Quilting satisfies this drive in many ways. Of course, quilts provide warmth to those in our care. More than that though, quiltmaking cracks open the door to the future and allows us to think ahead to our dreams for our descendants. Making quilts is, in a sense, a way for us to influence the future. A quilt says, "I was here. I loved you before you even existed."

Quilting provides us with the opportunity to create something of lasting beauty; but much more, it can carry our message of love and tenderness into the future. A quilt is laden with silent but powerful messages of patience, caring, friendship, and sharing. The quilts in this book were designed to be easy to make, straightforward, and uncomplicated. Many were created with just squares and rectangles. Some have many pieces, but all the pieces are simple. And all the quilts gave us the chance to play with color, value, pattern, and rhythm, and to send that little message of love into the future.

Introduction

THE QUILT PLANS in this book are arranged in groups according to the shapes of their pieces. The quilts in the first half of the book consist of squares and rectangles. If you are a brand-new quilter, we suggest you start with a small quilt and simple shapes. Read the sections on cutting and stitching blocks and assembling a quilt top. The section on finishing will help you complete your project.

If you are an experienced quiltmaker, you may want (or be expected) to provide quilts for family members for special days or momentous occasions. The quilts in this book are just what you need: adorable quilts designed for rotary cutting and speed sewing.

We have provided tips to help you cut and sew with precision. Read the tips to improve your accuracy, but keep in mind that quilting is a form of recreation and an opportunity for expression.

You will enjoy your quilt if it is accurately sewn, but don't let perfection become your only goal. Our "simple joys of quilting" are best described as pattern and rhythm, color and value, creation and expression, friendship and sharing. Take pleasure in these simple joys and use the quilt plans in the book. Feel free to add your personal touch. Your individual creativity and the work of your hands will transform any quilt into your own little masterpiece.

Rotary-Cutting Basics

THE ROTARY CUTTER is to quilting what the remote control is to football. It's the cleverness, cunning, and trickery of creating quilts that appeals to us as quiltmakers. Rotary-cutting equipment has revolutionized the process of both cutting and sewing pieces for quilts. Quilters can cut more layers of fabric with more accuracy and speed using a rotary cutter than they can using a pair of scissors.

Safety First

WHETHER YOU are using rotary equipment for the first time or are already an old pro, get into the habit of following a few precautions. The rotary blade is extremely sharp, and before you notice, you can unintentionally cut something important—like yourself.

* Always push the blade guard into place whenever you finish your cut. Keep the nut tight enough so that the guard will not slide back unintentionally.

* If you have children (under 20), keep your cutter in a safe place when not in use.

* Always roll the cutter away from you.

* If you have trouble with the ruler shifting as you cut, try cutting about 8" or 10" and then walking your hand forward on the ruler before cutting the next few inches. As soon as the cutter reaches the fabric next to your fingertips, stop and walk your hand forward on the ruler again.

Cutting Strips

CUTTING STRIPS at an exact right angle to the folded edge of your fabric is the backbone to cutting accurate strips. This starts with the first cut, known as the cleanup cut.

1. After prewashing, fold your fabric in half with the selvages together and press. Place the fabric on your cutting mat with the selvages toward you, and the fold even with a horizontal line at the top of the cutting mat. Place a 6" x 24" acrylic ruler so that the raw edges of both layers of fabric are covered, and the lines of your ruler match up with the vertical grid on your mat. Rolling the cutter away from you, cut from the selvages to the fold. Remove the ruler and gently remove the waste strip.

2. As you make additional cuts, align the desired strip measurement on the ruler with the cut edge of the fabric. Use the grid lines on your mat to double-check that you are making accurate cuts. After cutting three or four strips, realign the fold of your fabric with the lines on your mat and make a new cleanup cut.

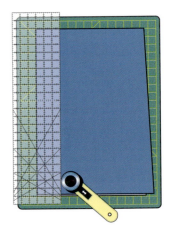

Sewing Basics

Conquering the ¼" Seam

SEWING AN exact ¼" seam is a simple skill and the key to successful quiltmaking. A presser foot with the right-hand edge of the foot exactly ¼" from the needle makes sewing an exact ¼" seam much easier. Your hands can keep the fabric feeding through the machine along the edge of the presser foot. If your machine does not have such a foot, you can do what many master quilters do—construct a little "fence" of masking tape that keeps the edge of the fabric exactly ¼" from the needle.

1. Place your ruler under your presser foot and slide it around until the needle is right above the ¼" line on the right-hand side of the ruler. Lower the needle until it sits right on that ¼" line. Fuss with the ruler until it's perfectly straight where it overlaps the rest of the machine.

2. Make a thick guide to help you sew a perfect ¼". We like something that is thick enough to keep the fabric from jumping the fence and riding off on its own little adventure. Layer five strips of 4"- or 5"-long masking tape on your cutting mat, one piece right on top of the other. You now have a piece of slightly chubby masking tape.

3. Look at the area to the right of the ruler, which is still under your needle and presser foot. If the feed dogs of your machine extend out to the right of the presser foot, use a pencil to draw a little notch on the masking-tape fence. Draw the notch about the same size as the exposed feed dogs. Use paper scissors to cut away the notch area.

4. Using the ruler as a guide, lay the stacked masking tape on the bed of the sewing machine so that most of the masking tape is aligned with the right-hand side of the ruler.

5. The guide is the portion of the tape without the notch. Because the tape is thick, it is easy for the fabric to stay on track.

Set the stitch-length dial on your sewing machine to about 12 stitches per inch (written as 2.5 on many machines).

Starting to Stitch

AFTER PERFECTING the ¼" seam, the next step in your learning process is remembering to hold on to the threads as you start stitching. Get in the habit of organizing yourself in a starting position as an Olympic athlete would. Align the two fabrics you are stitching and place them under the presser foot. Lower the presser foot, place your right hand behind the needle, and hold on to the two threads while the machine sews the first few stitches.

Chain Sewing

THIS IS a simple technique that will save you much time.

1. Organize all the pieces that are to be joined with right sides together in a stack with the side to be sewn on the right. Start with the same edge on each pair and the same color

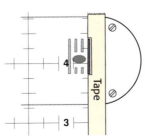

A True Beginner

Conquering the ¼" seam reminds me of an event in a class I taught several years ago. A darling, middle-aged quilting student announced to all of us that this was the first time she had ever sewn anything and that she was very excited about making a "queen-size quilt in a five-hour class."

My heart sank, but I suggested that she set up her gear and start practicing just sewing a straight line while I got the rest of the class started on the project of the day. As I was explaining the chief principle of the class, she came up, quite annoyed that her (borrowed) machine would not sew a straight line. I assured her that this skill would come with a bit more practice.

After I had the rest of the class settled and started, I went to this woman's table to give her some encouragement. Indeed, her seams ran wildly all over the fabric, with the seam allowances ranging from a ¹⁄₁₆" to 7". "Show me what you are doing," I suggested.

She lined up the two pieces of fabric, placed them under the needle, and carefully lowered the presser foot. Then, putting her right hand on one hip and her left hand on the other hip, she floored the foot pedal! That fabric shot through the machine at about seventy miles an hour and zoomed forward over the table in front of hers, landing about fifteen feet away. Needless to say, we all had a great laugh, and in no time she was sewing perfect ¼" seams. She has since become an avid quilter and always stitches with her little ¼" "fence" of masking tape. —JH

---

on top; this will help avoid confusion.

2. Sew each pair of fabrics one at a time without cutting the threads in between. Your work will look a bit like the flags at an amusement park.

3. Take the chain of pieces to the ironing board and snip the pairs apart as you press them.

Sewing with Accuracy

OPPOSING SEAMS

Rather than pressing seams open, quilters press the seams to one side, usually toward the darker color. The instructions may tell you to press the seams in opposite directions or toward a particular shape or color to make it easier for you to match the points or corners. This creates what we call opposing seams.

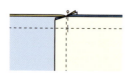

X MARKS THE SPOT

When pairs of triangles are sewn together, the stitching lines should cross each other on the back, creating an X. As you sew triangle units to other units, sew with the triangle units on top, and aim your stitching through the X. This will maintain the crisp points on your triangles.

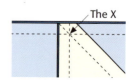

The X

EASING

If a fabric piece is shorter than the one it is supposed to match, pin the places where the two pieces should match and place them under your presser foot with the shorter one on top. The feed dogs, combined with a gentle tug on the fabrics, will help ease the two pieces together.

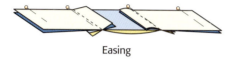

Easing

Another method for easing two uneven pieces together is to pin the seams with thin pins parallel to the seam edge; in other words, pin right on the seam line. Use very thin pins and stick the pins in and out two or three times as shown. Then sew slowly; pull the pins out at the very last second. This method will usually work when all else fails.

Pinning Long Seams

THE LONG seams of a block, where there are seams and points to match, must be pinned. Begin by pinning the matching points (where seam lines or points meet). Once these important points are firmly in place, pin the rest of the seam. Pull pins out of the seam line just before the needle hits them.

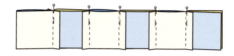

Machine Basting

SEWING PAIRS of triangles together can be difficult, especially when the pieces that meet have two different angles, such as in "Contrary Wife and Ornery Husband" on page 88.

Set the stitch length on your machine for as long a stitch as possible. Place the two seams to be matched together under the presser foot and hold them in place with a stiletto or the pointed end of a seam ripper. Machine baste the two seams. When the seams match correctly, sew them with a normal stitch length.

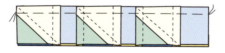

Baste.

Pressing

PRECISE PIECING is a combination of accurate sewing and gentle pressing. Frequent light pressing enables you to see where the pieces should be matched. Press often but lightly.

The traditional rule is to press seams to one side, toward the darker color whenever possible. Side-pressed seams add strength to the quilt, evenly distribute the bulk of the fabrics, and prevent the darker fabrics from showing through the lighter ones. Press the seam on the wrong side first, then turn the piece over and press from the right side.

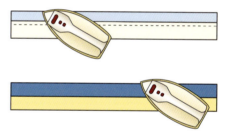

Pressing arrows are included when it is necessary to press the seams in a particular direction.

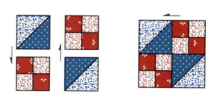

When no arrows are indicated, the direction of the seam allowance doesn't matter.

Unsewing

As we all know, mistakes do happen, and for one reason or another, stitches need to be removed. Until they invent an "unsew" feature on sewing machines like the backspace key on computers, you will need to use a seam ripper.

THE SEAM RIPPER

If you have a short line of stitching to remove, use an ordinary seam ripper. Slip the long point of the ripper under one stitch and slide the point further under the stitch until the sharp curve of the ripper cuts the thread. Cut every third or fourth stitch on straight-grain edges; cut every stitch on a bias edge. Pull the seam apart gently.

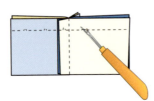

THE POWER SEAM RIPPER

A battery-operated mustache trimmer makes an unbelievable seam ripper. Use your regular seam ripper to slit the first three or four stitches in an errant seam. Then place the piece to be ripped on your thigh. Lift the upper fabric and slide the mustache trimmer between the two pieces of fabric. Press down gently on the lower fabric and move the trimmer forward. You can rip a pair of 42" strips in less than 60 seconds.

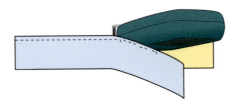

Using Piecing-Order Diagrams

A PIECING-ORDER diagram shows you the steps in which to join the pieces of your block. When quilters make a block, they sew small shapes to each other to make larger shapes. For example, when two right triangles are joined, they form a square. When two squares are joined, they form a rectangle.

These larger shapes, in turn, are sewn together to create the block. In general, try to sew in an order that allows you to sew progressively longer straight lines.

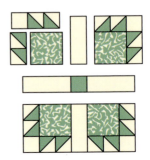

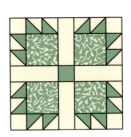

Clever Piecing Techniques

QUILTMAKERS HAVE devised clever strip-cutting and strip-piecing techniques to use with rotary equipment. While we call these techniques speed piecing, precise piecing would be a much more accurate name.

If you stitch several strips of fabric together to make a strip set and then cut across it, you can eliminate about half the time it would take to cut and sew squares individually. Of course, nonquilters don't grasp this at all. They only see the hundreds of squares and rectangles and think that you are a quilting queen, far superior to mere mortal beings. However, the quilts are beautiful and a joy to make.

Making Strip Sets

1. Cut strips the size called for in your quilt plan, and arrange them in the order they will be sewn together.

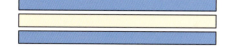

2. Sew the strips into strip sets.

3. Cut across the strips to create the segments.

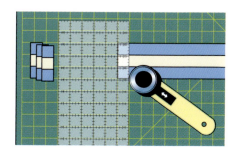

Sewing Big Triangle Blocks

BLOCKS MADE from pairs of large triangles are another example of quilters' cunning and trickery. These blocks make wonderful alternating blocks because they fill in space. They also establish a direction of design and create an illusion of depth. In "The Permanent Incomplete" on page 58, the large triangles zoom upward to the left while the easy little pieced blocks march upward to the right. To make large triangles like these, use the following easy formula and sewing technique.

1. Measure the finished size of the square created by the two triangles. Add ⅞" inch to the size of the square. (Remember that ⅞" is just a little bit less than an inch.) Each quilt plan

in this book will tell you how big to cut these pieces.

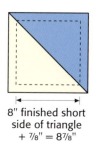

8" finished short
side of triangle
+ ⅞" = 8⅞"

2. Cut squares of each color in the size determined in step 1. Cut the squares once diagonally to make two half-square triangles of each color.

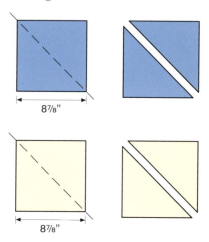

8⅞"

8⅞"

3. Place a light-colored triangle right sides together with a dark colored one and sew them together with a ¼" seam allowance. That's it!

Making Folded-Corner Triangles

THE FOLDED-CORNER technique is so easy it is almost embarrassing. Please don't tell nonquilters about this. We don't want them to know how simple this is and we certainly don't want them to know we have so much fun. Let them think of us as remarkably patient and generous, willing to slave away to show our love and devotion. Clever quilters have devised this ingenious trick using small squares with larger squares or rectangles.

1. Fold a square in half on the diagonal and press a crease along the fold. (Each quilt plan will tell you how big to cut the squares and rectangles.)

Fold and crease.

2. Place the pressed square on the corner of a square as shown. Sew along the crease. Trim away the extra fabric, ¼" from the seam line. Press the triangle toward the corner.

3. Repeat for the remaining corners.

Making Half-Square Triangle Units

WHEN YOU draw a line on a square from corner to corner and cut the square in half, you create two equal triangles. We call this pair of triangles "half-square triangles." When you read the phrase "half-square triangle units," we mean two equal triangles that create one square.

Simple squares and rectangles provide us with countless beautiful designs, but adding half-square triangle units unleashes thousands of design and pattern possibilities. Since half-square triangle units are such a fabulous design element and so important for advancing your quilting skills, we'll explain an easy, quick, and accurate way to make large numbers of them.

FABRIC GRAIN

The grain of fabric is very important. Fabric is woven of threads that cross each other at right angles. The long sides of the fabric have a finished edge that is called the selvage. The direction that the threads run in a fabric is called the grain. The threads that run the length of the fabric, parallel to the selvage, make up the lengthwise grain. The crosswise grain runs from side to side, perpendicular to the selvage. Both the lengthwise and crosswise grains are often referred to as straight grain.

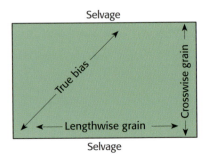

The diagonal of a woven fabric is called the bias. True bias runs at a 45° angle to the length and width of the fabric. Learning to cut strips on the bias grain gives you an unexpected advantage. You can sew the bias strips together and then cut squares from the sewn strips that have perfect straight grain on the outside!

CUTTING AND SEWING THE STRIPS

1. To determine the width of the strip to cut, measure the finished short side of the triangle. Add ½" to that measurement. This measurement will be the width of your bias strips. For example, if the finished short side of the triangle is 2", add ½" to the 2" and cut a strip 2½" wide.

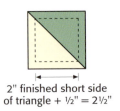

2" finished short side of triangle + ½" = 2½"

2. Cut one square from the background fabric and one from the contrasting fabric. The quilt directions will tell you what size square to cut. Layer both squares right side up. Place the layered fabrics on your cutting mat.

3. Cut the squares diagonally from corner to corner, then cut bias strips the width determined in step 1. Each quilt plan will tell you how wide to cut the strips.

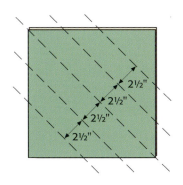

4. With right sides together, sew the strips into a unit, alternating the colors. Offset the tops exactly ¼" so that the top of the unit of strips forms a straight line. Press toward the darker color. Repeat for the second set of strips.

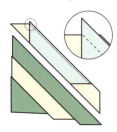

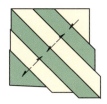

CUTTING THE SEGMENTS

1. Place a ruler with the bias line on one of the middle seam lines in your unit, and trim the edge of the unit so that it is at a perfect 45° angle with the seam line. At the risk of sounding like terrible fussbudgets, we must repeat that for this method to be accurate, you must retrim the side of the unit before cutting each segment.

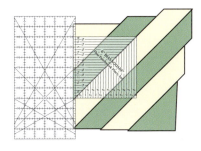

2. Cut a segment from the unit the exact size of the cut square. Cut carefully because you are actually cutting the second side of each square. Cut the segments ½" larger than the finished square. For example, if the finished square is 2", add ½" to that measurement and cut the segment 2½" wide.

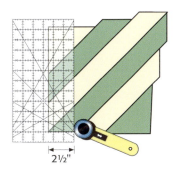

3. Repeat step 1 to trim the side of the unit to a perfect 45° angle with the seams. Then cut another segment. Continue to trim the unit to a perfect 45° angle and cut segments until you have cut up the entire unit of strips.

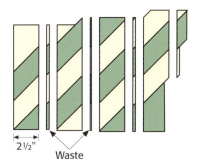

CUTTING THE SQUARES

1. Use a ruler with a bias line to cut the segment into squares. Position the edge of the ruler on the edge of the fabric, and the diagonal line of the ruler on the seam line.

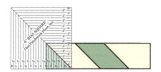

2. With the ruler properly positioned, cut along the right-hand side of every seam in the segment.

3. Turn the mat around to place all the right-hand cuts at your left. Reposition the ruler so the edge of the ruler is on the edge of the fabric and the diagonal line is on the seam line, and trim the pieces to perfect squares.

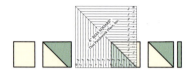

Making Quarter-Square Triangle Units

As QUILTERS, we all love the amazing and clever techniques thought up by our colleagues and friends. Where do these creative ideas come from—cutting strips of fabric to make squares, sewing folded corners, making half-square triangle units, using mustache trimmers as rippers? These ideas are really clever and great fun. But the idea of making quarter-square triangle units from half-square triangle units—well, this is flabbergasting. With these triangles, which are one-quarter of a square, you can make many intricate patterns more accurately and easily.

The method is almost the same as the one for making half-square triangle units. Cutting the strips, the segments, and the units to prepare for the quarter-square triangle units is the same. The only difference is that after you cut the half-square triangle units, you simply cut them in half, sew two halves of the appropriate colors together, and—voilá—you have a quarter-square triangle unit ready to be sewn into a block.

CUTTING THE STRIPS AND SEGMENTS

1. Cut one square from background fabric and one from contrasting fabric. Each quilt plan will tell you what size square to cut. Layer both fabrics right side up. Place the layered fabrics on the cutting mat.

2. To determine the strip width to cut, measure the finished long side of a triangle in the quarter-square unit. Add ⅞" to that measurement. For most quilts, this measurement should be the width of your bias strips. For example, if the finished long side of the triangle is 3", add ⅞" to the 3" for a strip width of 3⅞".

3" finished long
side of triangle
+ ⅞" = 3⅞"

3. Referring to the directions for "Cutting and Sewing the Strips" and "Cutting the Segments" on pages 12–13, cut the strips and segments. In most cases, the segments are cut the same width as the bias strips. Using our example above of cutting 3⅞"-wide strips, we would then cut the segments 3⅞" wide. Each quilt plan will tell you how wide to cut the strips and segments.

CUTTING THE HALF-SQUARE TRIANGLE UNITS AND SEWING QUARTER-SQUARE TRIANGLE UNITS

1. Follow the directions on pages 13 and 14 to cut the half-square triangle units. Cut the units ⅞" larger than the finished square. If the finished square is 3", cut the unit 3⅞". Now, place your ruler diagonally on the half-square triangle unit and cut the square in half.

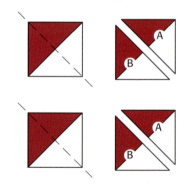

2. Arrange and sew the two halves together to form the quarter-square triangle unit.

Assembling the Quilt Top

WHAT A SATISFYING feeling to have finished making all your blocks! Now it is time to arrange them into rows and put the quilt top together. The best way to arrange the blocks is on your design wall. A design wall can be a piece of flannel or thin batting tacked to a wall, or it can be one or two sheets of 4' x 8' insulation board covered with flannel.

After arranging the blocks, sashings, setting squares, side and corner triangles, or whatever your quilt has, stand back and squint at your arrangement (a reducing glass may also be used). Are the colors evenly distributed? Does it match the quilt diagram? Are you pleased with how it looks? Good. As you sew the rows together, take down one row at a time, replacing it when it is stitched together; it is easy to get confused as to what row you are working on.

Making Straight-Set Quilts

THE BLOCKS in a straight-set quilt are arranged in straight rows and are easy to assemble.

1. Arrange the blocks in rows as shown in the quilt-assembly diagram for your project, adding sashings and/or setting squares if applicable.

2. Sew the blocks together in horizontal rows. Press the seams in opposite directions from one row to the next, unless instructed otherwise. For example, if you have two

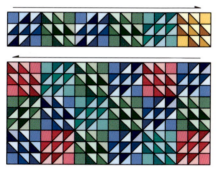

Press seams in opposite directions from row to row.

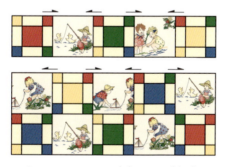

Press seams toward the same block.

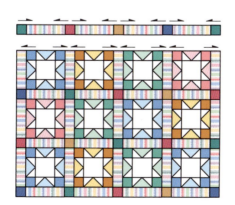

Press seams toward the sashing strips.

blocks that alternate with each other in your quilt, press all the seams toward the same block; or if you have sashings in your quilt, press all the seams either toward or away from the sashings. Pressing arrows in the quilt-assembly diagrams indicate the direction to press the seams.

3. Carefully pin or machine baste the seams between the blocks from one row to the next and sew the rows together. Press the seams between the rows in one direction.

Making Diagonal-Set Quilts

THE BLOCKS for a diagonal-set quilt are placed on-point and arranged in diagonal rows. Corner and side setting triangles are then added to fill in the side and corner spaces. When blocks are set diagonally or on-point, the bias grain runs horizontally and vertically, which can result in a quilt top that sags. To stabilize the edges of the quilt, you'll need to cut the corner and side triangles so that the side of the triangles placed along the edge are on the straight grain.

The squares for these corner and side triangles are cut slightly oversized to make sewing them to the quilt easier. They will be trimmed before borders are added. Each quilt plan will tell you how large to cut these squares.

CORNER SETTING TRIANGLES

When you cut a square in half *once* on the diagonal, you create two triangles that have the straight of grain on the short sides. Sew these triangles to the corners of a diagonally set quilt.

SIDE SETTING TRIANGLES

When you cut a square in half *twice* on the diagonal, you produce four triangles that have the straight of grain on the long side of each triangle. Sew these triangles along the sides and top and bottom edges of a diagonally set quilt.

ASSEMBLING A DIAGONAL SETTING

1. Arrange the blocks, side setting triangles, and corner setting triangles as shown in the quilt-assembly diagram for your project.

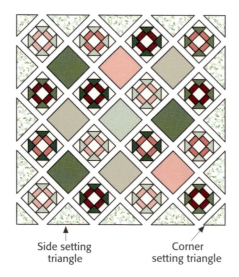

Side setting triangle

Corner setting triangle

2. Sew the blocks and side triangles together in diagonal rows. Press the seams in opposite directions from one row to the next. If you have two different alternating blocks within the rows, press all the seams toward the same block.

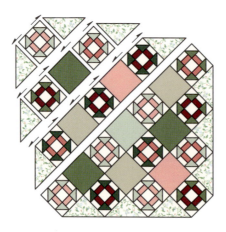

3. Carefully pin or machine baste the seams between the blocks from one row to the next. Sew the diagonal rows together. Press the seams between the rows in one direction. Add the corner setting triangles last.

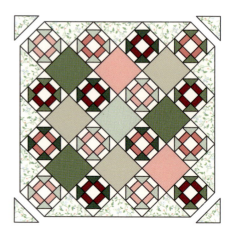

4. Because the corner and side triangles are slightly oversized, you will need to trim the edges of the quilt. Align the ¼" mark on your ruler with the points of the blocks and trim the edges ¼" from these points. In some cases, you will be instructed to trim more than ¼" from the points. This extra fabric between the points and the edge of the quilt is called float and gives the appearance the blocks are floating on the background.

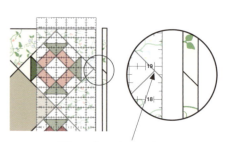

Align ¼" mark on ruler with block point. Trim.

Adding Borders

MANY QUILTS are transformed by the frame that a border provides. Quilt borders, like frames, can grab your eyes and focus them on the center blocks of a quilt. Borders emphasize and give significance to the designs they surround. Whether plain strips of fabric or rows of piecing, thoughtfully planned and sewn borders may greatly enhance a quilt. The best way to decide whether your quilt will benefit by a border is to experiment with a few variations.

Well-designed borders echo the color, size, and shapes of the pieces in the blocks. If the borders are pieced, the shapes of the pieces should have some relationship to the shapes in the blocks. Notice that the red triangles in the border of "Red Union Square" on page 110 are the same size and shape as the triangles used in the blocks.

The single most important thing to remember about borders is that they must be cut to fit the actual size of the center of the quilt top, not the outer edges. It is also important that the quilt end up "square," with 90-degree corners and with opposite sides equal to each other. First, cut border strips longer than you think you'll need. Later, trim them to fit the measurements of the center of the quilt.

JOINING BORDER STRIPS

The fabric requirements for the borders in this book are based on cutting the border strips on the crosswise grain. Cut strips as indicated in the cutting directions for your quilt. If the quilt is larger than 42", sew the strips together, end to end, with a straight or diagonal seam. Measure the quilt as shown and trim the long strips to the appropriate lengths.

Straight seam

Diagonal seam

STRAIGHT-SEWN BORDERS

Measure and cut border strips, following the steps below. By encouraging the quilt to fit the measured strips, you ensure that the quilt will be square with flat borders. This is an important step, so resist the temptation to skip it. You may have to ease one side of a quilt to fit a border and stretch the opposite side slightly to fit the same dimension. Press all border seams away from the center of the quilt top or toward the border unless instructed otherwise.

Borders with Straight-Sewn Corners

1. Measure the length of the quilt at the center. Trim two of the border strips to that measurement. Sew these strips to the sides of the quilt, easing as necessary.

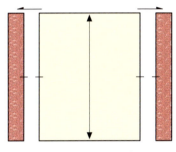

Measure center of quilt, top to bottom.

2. Measure the width of the quilt at the center, including the side borders and seam allowances as shown. Cut the borders to this length and sew them to the top and bottom of the quilt, easing as necessary.

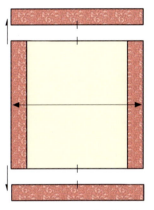

Measure center of quilt, side to side, including borders.

If your quilt has several strips of plain borders with straight-sewn corners, follow the same order as outlined above, sewing the sides first and then the top and bottom.

Straight-Sewn Borders with Corner Squares

1. Measure the length of the quilt at the center. Trim two of the border strips to that measurement. Measure the width of the quilt at the center, and trim the top and bottom border strips to this measurement.

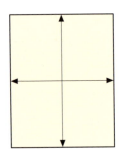

2. Sew the strips to the sides first, easing as necessary.

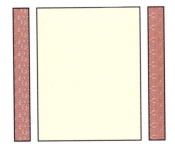

3. Sew a corner square to each end of the top and bottom strips, and sew these to the quilt, easing as necessary.

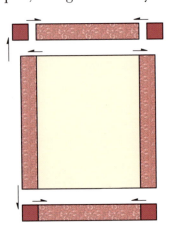

If your quilt has several strips of plain borders with corner squares, follow the same order as outlined above.

PIECED BORDERS

Pieced borders take your quilt to a higher level of craftsmanship. Occasionally, you may need to add a "coping" strip to the quilt top to make the pieced border fit perfectly. Notice the "Red Union Square" quilt on page 110. The pieced blocks in the diagonal setting required adding a 1"-wide red strip to the red setting triangles to create the perfect size for the sawtooth border. The quilt plan will tell you how big to make your coping strip if one is required.

← Pieced border

Coping strip

BORDERS WITH MITERED CORNERS

Quilts with three or four border strips often look better and are easier to sew if they have mitered corners.

NOTE: *If your quilt has multiple borders, center your border strips on each other and sew them together. This makes it easier to match the fabrics on the corners and simplifies sewing the strips to the quilt top. Treat the joined multiple borders as a single unit.*

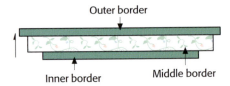

Outer border

Inner border

Middle border

1. Measure the length of the quilt through the center, from seam line to seam line. Measure the finished width of the border strips. Double this measurement, and add it to the length of the quilt top. Add an extra 4" just in case. For example:

Length of quilt = 60"
8"-wide border x 2 = 16"
Plus extra = 4"
Total = 80"

2. Follow step 1 to cut the top and bottom borders, except measure the width of the quilt through the center and add the doubled measurement of the border strips to the width of the quilt top. Don't forget to add the extra 4".

3. Measure the width and length of the quilt through the center, from seam line to seam line (not including seam allowances). Use a small ruler to measure and pinpoint the ¼" seam allowance on each corner of your quilt.

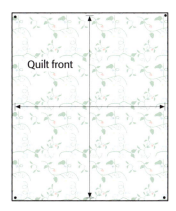

Measure seam line to seam line *not* including seam allowances.

4. Using the width and length measurement of the quilt (as measured in step 3), mark the seam lines on each set of border strips with pins. Fold the border strips in half; pin to mark the center.

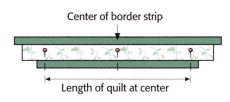

Center of border strip

Length of quilt at center

5. Fold the quilt top in half; use pins to mark the center of each of the sides and top and bottom of the quilt.

6. Center the border strip on the side of the quilt, so that the strip extends an equal distance beyond each end of the quilt top. Pin the border to the quilt, matching the centers, ends, and important points. Generously pin the rest of the border to the quilt. Make the quilt fit the guide pins in the borders.

7. Sew the borders to the quilt top with a ¼" seam, starting and ending ¼" from the edge of the quilt and backstitching at both ends. In other words, leave the first and last ¼" unsewn. Add the other three strips in the same manner.

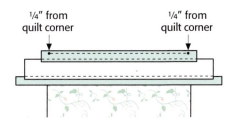

¼" from quilt corner

¼" from quilt corner

8. Arrange the border strips on either side of the corner so that they are lined up and the rest of your quilt top is folded diagonally.

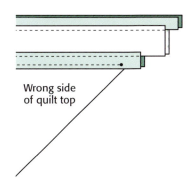

Wrong side of quilt top

9. Using a pencil and a 6" x 24" acrylic ruler with a 45° angle printed on it, mark a 45° angle on the wrong side of each strip, starting at the intersection of the seam lines as shown below.

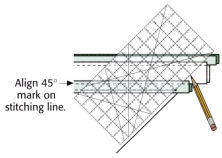

Align 45° mark on stitching line.

Draw line from seam intersection to outer edge of borders.

10. Pin carefully, matching the marked lines. Sew along the lines, backstitching at both ends. Trim the seams to ¼" and press open.

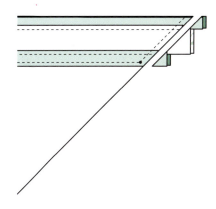

Squares and Rectangles

White and Blue, Old and New

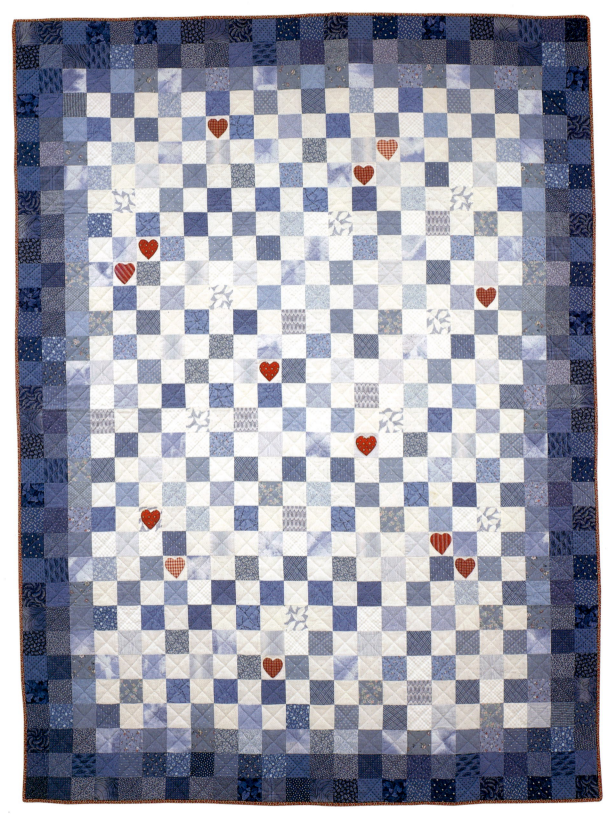

WHITE AND BLUE, OLD AND NEW by Mary Hickey, Keyport, Washington, 1995.
Hand quilted by the Amish of Millersburg, Ohio.

I have seen and made many blue-and-white quilts in the last twenty years. However, my favorites are always the simplest ones. Plain white squares, alternating with a variety of blue squares, create a simple directness that is very endearing.

Gather your friends and beg, borrow, and plead for 3½"-wide strips of blue fabric. You will have a great variety of blues for your quilt and a scrap of true-blue love from each of your friends. The strips can be very short, even just one square. Make the center of the quilt in sixteen-patch blocks of blue and white squares. The border is just more sixteen-patch blocks in medium and dark blues. Toss on a baker's dozen of red hearts, and you have a fresh, sweet quilt, guaranteed to lift your heart every time you see it. —MH

NOTE: *We have written the directions using 21"-long strips of fabric. This will enable you to strip-piece your blocks and still obtain many different shades of blue and white. If you are working with smaller scraps of fabric, make strips sets with similar lengths, cut segments, and join them to make the sixteen-patch blocks. If your scraps are very small, cut 3½" squares and sew 16 alternating blue and white squares together.*

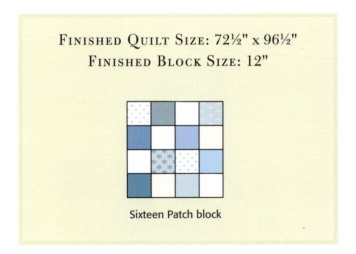

FINISHED QUILT SIZE: 72½" x 96½"
FINISHED BLOCK SIZE: 12"

Sixteen Patch block

Materials 42"-wide fabric

* 2¾ yds. *total* assorted white and muslin fabrics*
* 3¼ yds. *total* assorted light and medium-light blue fabrics
* 1⅛ yds. *total* assorted medium blue fabrics
* 1⅛ yds. *total* assorted medium-dark blue fabrics
* ¾ yd. *total* assorted dark blue fabrics
* ⅜ yd. red print for hearts
* 5¾ yds. for backing
* 77" x 101" piece of batting
* ¾ yd. for binding

*Select solid muslin and white fabrics as well as light blue prints on muslin or white backgrounds.

Cutting

ALL MEASUREMENTS include ¼"-wide seam allowances.

From the assorted white and muslin fabrics, cut:
* 48 strips, 3½" x 21"
* 2 squares, 3½" x 3½"

From the assorted light/medium-light blue fabrics, cut:
* 56 strips, 3½" x 21"
* 14 squares, 3½" x 3½"

From the assorted medium blue fabrics, cut:
- 16 strips, 3½" x 21"
- 12 squares, 3½" x 3½"

From the assorted medium-dark blue fabrics, cut:
- 16 strips, 3½" x 21"
- 24 squares, 3½" x 3½"

From the assorted dark blue fabrics, cut:
- 8 strips, 3½" x 21"
- 12 squares, 3½" x 3½"

From the red print, cut:
- 26 squares, 3½" x 3½", for hearts

Making the Blocks

1. Sew 3½" x 21" strips of white, light/medium-light blue strips together as shown to make strip set A. Make 24 strip sets. Crosscut the strip sets into 116 segments, 3½" wide.

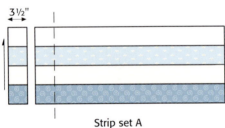

Strip set A
Make 24. Cut a total of 116 segments.

2. Assemble 4 A segments as shown to make a center block. Make 24 blocks. Reserve the remaining 20 A segments for the border blocks.

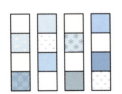

Center blocks
Make 24.

3. Sew 3½" x 21" strips of light/medium-light blue and medium blue together as shown to make strip set B. Make 4 strip sets. Crosscut the strip sets into 20 segments, 3½" wide.

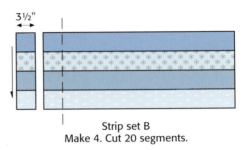

Strip set B
Make 4. Cut 20 segments.

4. Sew 3½" x 21" strips of medium blue and medium dark blue together as shown to make strip set C. Make 4 strip sets. Crosscut the strips sets into 20 segments, 3½" wide.

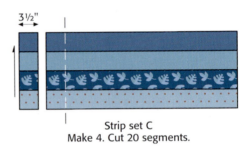

Strip set C
Make 4. Cut 20 segments.

5. Sew 3½" x 21" strips of medium dark blue and dark blue together as shown to make strip set D. Make 4 strips sets. Crosscut the strip sets into 20 segments, 3½" wide.

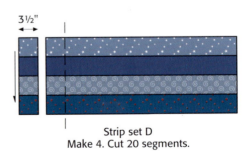

Strip set D
Make 4. Cut 20 segments.

6. Assemble the A, B, C, and D strips as shown to make a border block. Make 10 Border 1 blocks, and 10 Border 2 blocks.

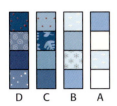

D   C   B   A

Border 1 block
Make 10.

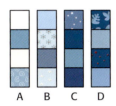

A   B   C   D

Border 2 block
Make 10.

7. Assemble 16 assorted 3½" squares as shown to make a corner block. Make 2 Corner 1 blocks and 2 Corner 2 blocks.

Corner 1 block
Make 2.

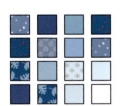

Corner 2 block
Make 2.

Making the Hearts: Face-and-Turn Appliqué

1. Trace the heart shape (on page 26) onto template plastic or cardboard and cut a template of the heart.

2. Using a water-soluble pen, trace the heart onto 13 of the 3½" red squares.

3. With right sides together, place a marked red square on top of another red square and sew on the drawn line. Use a very small stitch—1.5 or 1.0 on a European machine or 16 on an American machine. Carefully trim away the excess fabric, leaving only a scant ⅛" seam allowance.

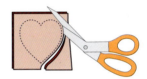

4. Cut a slit about 1¼" long in the back of the heart only.

5. Spray the heart lightly with water and turn the heart right side out. Use the end of a chopstick to smooth the points and inner corners. Press the hearts. Appliqué one heart on a white square in 13 of the center 16-patch blocks.

Make 13.

Assembling the Quilt Top

1. Referring to the diagram below, arrange the blocks in 8 rows of 6 blocks each.

2. Referring to "Making Straight-Set Quilts" on page 15, pin and sew the blocks together in horizontal rows. Carefully pin and sew the rows together, matching the seams.

Corner 2 block	Border 1 block	Border 1 block	Border 1 block	Border 1 block	Corner 1 block
Border 1 block	Center block	Center block	Center block	Center block	Border 2 block
Border 1 block	Center block	Center block	Center block	Center block	Border 2 block
Border 1 block	Center block	Center block	Center block	Center block	Border 2 block
Border 1 block	Center block	Center block	Center block	Center block	Border 2 block
Border 1 block	Center block	Center block	Center block	Center block	Border 2 block
Border 1 block	Center block	Center block	Center block	Center block	Border 2 block
Corner 1 block	Border 2 block	Border 2 block	Border 2 block	Border 2 block	Corner 2 block

Finishing the Quilt

1. Layer the quilt top, batting, and backing; baste. Quilt as desired.

2. Trim the batting and backing even with the edges of the quilt top. Sew the binding to the edges of the quilt.

3. Make and attach a label to your finished quilt.

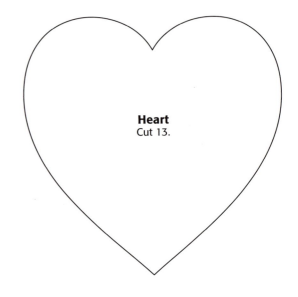

Heart
Cut 13.

Amish Trip Around the World

AMISH TRIP AROUND THE WORLD, pieced and hand quilted by the Amish of Shipshewana, Indiana, 1994.

One autumn, in the early 1990s, an Amish family invited me to teach in their quilt shop in northern Indiana. My Amish friends picked me up at the airport and we trotted, clop clopping, through the enchanted landscape of soft hills and spectacular fall color into the village of Shipshewana.

I loved spending time with these kind and gentle people. I taught the "English" (non-Amish) women from Illinois, Indiana, and Michigan for two days, and then the Amish women on Saturday—all in the huge barn-loft classroom provided by the store. After classes on Saturday afternoon, I went across the road to a warehouse, where I watched as several families cooked and canned meat for the hungry in East Africa. In another building, buyers from New York were bidding on handmade quilts. The profits from the quilts were to be donated to a group of missionaries teaching in Viet Nam.

I bought this "Trip around the World" from my Amish friends to commemorate this wonderful trip. The colors are faint mimics of the sky, leaves, earth, and trees of this beautiful part of America and are the typical palette of the Midwestern Amish. The fabric combination symbolizes the community of good people, working out their lives in calmness and simplicity. —MH

NOTE: *Quilters are often teased about buying perfectly good fabric and cutting it up just to sew it back together. In this quilt, we go one step crazier, since we sew some seams just to rip them apart. But by doing this, we make the sewing of the squares in the proper order so easy it's automatic. (Well, almost!)*

FINISHED QUILT SIZE: 46" x 46"

Materials 42"-wide fabric

* ¼ yd. each of 2 shades of green solid
* ¼ yd. each of 2 shades of orange solid
* ¼ yd. golden yellow solid
* ¼ yd. dark blue solid
* ⅝ yd. medium blue solid for squares and inner border
* 1 yd. burgundy solid for squares and outer border
* 2⅞ yds. for backing
* 50" x 50" piece of batting
* ½ yd. for binding
* Seam ripper (Don't panic.)

Cutting

ALL MEASUREMENTS include ¼"-wide seam allowances.

From each of the green, orange, golden yellow, dark blue, medium blue, and burgundy solids, cut:

* 2 strips, 2½" x 42", from each color (16 strips total)
* 4* squares, 2½" x 2½", from each color, plus 1 more burgundy square (33 squares total)

From the medium blue solid, cut:

* 4 strips, 2½" x 42", for inner borders

From the burgundy solid, cut:

* 5 strips, 4¼" x 42", for outer borders

*If your strips are 44" long, you will be able to cut the necessary segments from the strip sets. In that case, you will only need 2 squares from each fabric, plus the extra burgundy square. See step 3.

Making the Trip Around the World

1. Choose the most predominant fabric (or the fabric you want to form the complete diagonal square or "trip"). Number the fabrics from 1 to 8, with your most predominant fabric as fabric 1; in our quilt, fabric 1 is the burgundy. Using 1 strip from each color, arrange and sew the 8 strips in numerical order. Make 2 identical strip sets.

Make 2 strip sets.

NOTE: *When sewing the strips together, sew every other row in the opposite direction to avoid having the strips curve into a rainbow.*

2. With right sides together, join the long edges of the strip set to form a tube. Repeat with the remaining strip set to make a second tube.

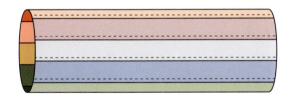

3. Lay one of the tubes, folded flat, on your mat. Carefully crosscut the tube into 16 segments (loops), 2½" wide. Repeat with the second tube. Cut a total of 32 loops.

NOTE: *If your strip tubes happen to be 44" wide, you will be able to cut 17 segments from each strip set, which is what you need. If you can cut a total*

of 34 segments from the strip tubes, go on to step 5. Otherwise, see step 4.

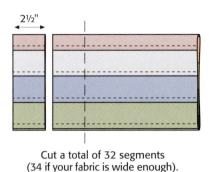

Cut a total of 32 segments
(34 if your fabric is wide enough).

S TOP AFTER *every third cut to make a new cleanup cut, to make sure your cuts are at a true right angle with the seams.*

---

4. If your strips are only 42" wide, you will only be able to cut a total of 32 segments from the strip tubes. Since you need 34 segments, you will need to join squares to make 2 additional segments. Using one square of each color, sew 8 squares together in the same order as the strip sets to make each of 2 segments. Use these segments for the center, row 9.

Make 2.

5. Use your seam ripper to open 1 loop between fabrics 1 and 8. Repeat with a second loop. Sew a fabric 1 square between the segments, with fabric 8 next to fabric 1, to make row 1. Repeat for rows 9 and 17.

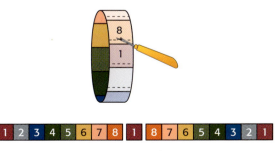

Rows 1, 9, and 17

6. Open the seam on 2 more loops between fabrics 1 and 2. Sew a fabric 2 square between the segments, with fabric 1 next to fabric 2 to make row 2. Repeat for row 16.

Rows 2 and 16

7. Repeat this process for each row as shown in the chart below, using 2 loops and 1 square for each row.

To Make Rows	Open Seam Between Fabrics	Sew Segments to Fabric Square
3 and 15	2 and 3	2 next to 3
4 and 14	3 and 4	3 next to 4
5 and 13	4 and 5	4 next to 5
6 and 12	5 and 6	5 next to 6
7 and 11	6 and 7	6 next to 7
8 and 10	7 and 8	7 next to 8

Assembling the Quilt Top

1. Referring to the diagram below, arrange the rows in numerical order. Press the seams in odd-numbered rows in one direction, and the seams in even-numbered rows in the opposite direction.

Row

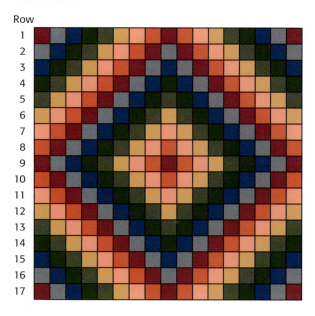

2. Sew the rows together in pairs, matching the seams. Press the seams in one direction. Join the pairs of rows to complete the center of the quilt.

3. Referring to "Joining Border Strips" on page 17, sew the border strips end to end. Referring to "Borders with Mitered Corners" on pages 18–19, sew the inner and outer border strips together. Make 4 border units. Sew the border units to the quilt top. Miter the corners.

Make 4.

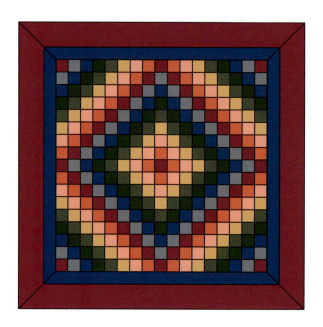

Finishing the Quilt

1. Layer the quilt top, batting, and backing; baste. Quilt as desired. Quilted in typical Trip around the World fashion, this quilt has single lines of stitching running diagonally through all the squares, and a cable design is quilted in the outer border.

2. Trim the batting and backing even with the edges of the quilt top. Sew the binding to the edges of the quilt.

3. Make and attach a label to your finished quilt.

Purple Passion

PURPLE PASSION by Joan Hanson, Seattle, Washington, 1985. From the collection of Preston and Suzanne Martin.

The strong visual appeal of this traditional Double Irish Chain pattern has made it a favorite for many generations. Strip-piecing techniques make it a speedy and accurate project for beginners and experienced quilters alike. If selecting fabrics is overwhelming to you, choosing two fabrics of the same color, one a bit darker than the other, is a way to simplify the fabric selection process. I made this version for my sister and brother-in-law as a wedding gift. The lavender fabrics were also used for the bridesmaid and flower-girl dresses, which adds to the sentimental value for the bride and groom. —JH

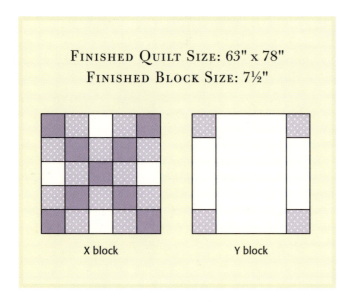

FINISHED QUILT SIZE: 63" x 78"
FINISHED BLOCK SIZE: 7½"

X block   Y block

Materials 42"-wide fabric

* 2⅞ yds. off-white solid for blocks and middle border
* 2 yds. light lavender print for blocks
* 1¼ yds. medium lavender print for blocks
* ¾ yd. dark lavender print for inner and outer borders
* 4 yds. for backing
* 67" x 82" piece of batting
* ¾ yd. dark lavender solid for binding

Cutting

ALL MEASUREMENTS include ¼"-wide seam allowances.

From the off-white solid, cut:
* 8 strips, 2" x 42", for X block
* 4 strips, 5" x 42", for Y block
* 4 strips, 8" x 42"; crosscut strips into 31 rectangles, 5" x 8", for Y block
* 8 strips, 3½" x 42", for middle border

From the light lavender print, cut:
* 32 strips, 2" x 42" (24 strips for X block, and 8 strips for Y block)

From the medium lavender print, cut:
* 18 strips, 2" x 42", for X block

From the dark lavender print, cut:
* 16 strips, 1½" x 42", for inner and outer borders

Making the Blocks

1. Sew the 2"-wide strips of off-white, light lavender, and medium lavender together as shown to make strip sets A, B, and C. Make 4 of strip set A, 4 of strip set B, and 2 of strip set C. Crosscut the A strip sets into 64 segments, 2" wide. Crosscut the B strip sets into 64 segments, 2" wide. Crosscut the C strip sets into 32 segments, 2" wide.

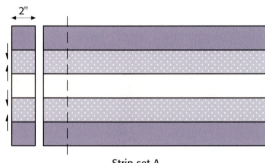

Strip set A
Make 4. Cut 64 segments.

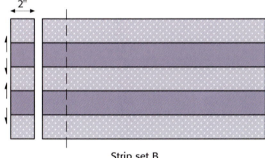

Strip set B
Make 4. Cut 64 segments.

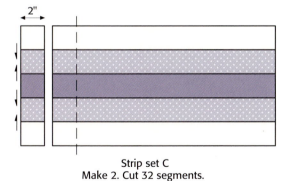

Strip set C
Make 2. Cut 32 segments.

2. Assemble the segments as shown to make block X. Make 32 blocks.

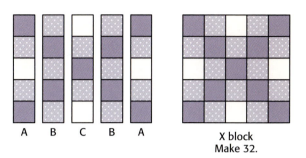

A   B   C   B   A   X block
                              Make 32.

3. Sew a 2"-wide light lavender strip to opposite sides of a 5"-wide off-white background strip as shown to make a strip set. Make 4 strip sets. Crosscut the strip sets into 62 segments, 2" wide.

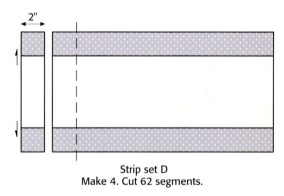

Strip set D
Make 4. Cut 62 segments.

4. Sew a segment from step 3 to opposite sides of a 5" x 8" background rectangle to make Y block. Make 31 blocks.

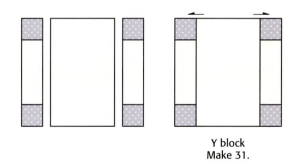

Y block
Make 31.

Assembling the Quilt Top

1. Referring to the diagram below, arrange the blocks in 9 horizontal rows of 7 blocks each.

2. Referring to "Making Straight-Set Quilts" on page 15, sew the blocks together into rows. Press the seams toward the X blocks. Carefully pin and sew the rows together, matching the seams.

3. Referring to "Joining Border Strips" on page 17, sew the border strips end to end. Referring to "Borders with Mitered Corners" on pages 18–19, sew the inner and outer border strips to opposite sides of the middle border strips. Make 4 border units. Sew the border units to the quilt top. Miter the corners.

Make 4.

Finishing the Quilt

1. Layer the quilt top, batting, and backing; baste. Quilt as desired.

2. Trim the batting and backing even with the edges of the quilt top. Sew the binding to the edges of the quilt.

3. Make and attach a label to your finished quilt.

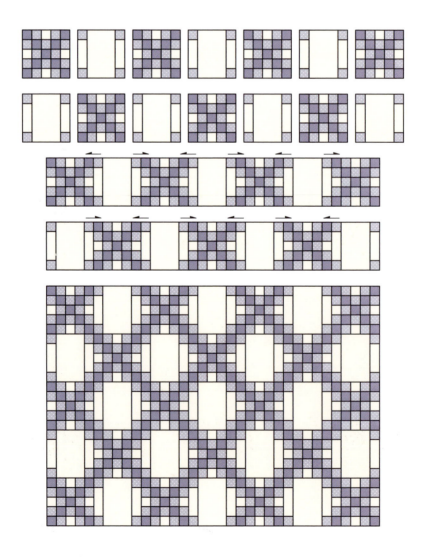

Lickity Split

LICKITY SPLIT by Mary Hickey, Seattle, Washington, 2000. Machine quilted by Frankie Schmitt.

As often happens, a tiny picture of a portion of an antique quilt in a book of country-style quilts and decorating inspired this color scheme. Vibrant red Stepping Stones blocks frame denim blue Town Square blocks. While both blocks measure 10", the blue blocks create a five-patch grid and the red blocks produce a six-patch grid. This unusual difference in a two-block quilt makes it easy to stitch the blocks into rows since the seams do not have to (in fact cannot possibly) match. Notice that the blues in the Town Square blocks are graded from dark on the outer edges to glowing pastel in the centers. Our sample incorporates red homespun plaids in the Stepping Stones blocks, but consider using a print or even a novelty fabric.

Do you want to make a big quilt quickly? These easy blocks made of squares and rectangles zoom together so quickly, you will be finished in no time. In fact, I planned this quilt and prepared the strip units to take to a friend's beach cabin. Like most beach cabins, the floor space was quite limited and I did not have room to spread out the quilt while I was working on it. Imagine my surprise when I got home and discovered that the quilt was a full two rows (20") longer than I had intended. Now that's an easy quilt! Notice also that by placing solid red squares at the corners of the quilt, you eliminate the problem of matching (or not matching) the plaid on the corners of the outer border. —MH

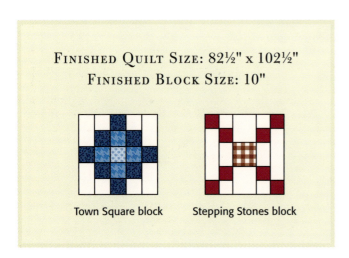

FINISHED QUILT SIZE: 82½" x 102½"
FINISHED BLOCK SIZE: 10"

Town Square block   Stepping Stones block

Materials 42"-wide fabric

* 4¼ yds. *total* assorted off-white prints for Town Square and Stepping Stones blocks
* ¼ yd. *total* assorted light blue prints for Town Square blocks
* ¾ yd. *total* assorted medium blue prints for Town Square blocks
* 1¼ yds. *total* assorted dark blue prints for Town Square blocks
* 1¼ yds. *total* assorted dark red prints for Stepping Stones blocks
* ¾ yd. dark red print for inner border and corner squares in outer border
* ⅜ yd. *total* assorted red plaids for Stepping Stones blocks
* 1¼ yds. red plaid for outer border
* 6¼ yds. for backing
* 87" x 107" piece of batting
* 1 yd. for binding

Cutting

ALL MEASUREMENTS include ¼"-wide seam allowances.

From the assorted off-white prints, cut:
- 8 strips, 4½" x 42", for Town Square blocks
- 8 strips, 2½" x 42", for Town Square blocks
- 4 strips, 7" x 42", for Stepping Stones blocks
- 8 strips, 2¼" x 42", for Stepping Stones blocks
- 4 strips, 3½" x 42", for Stepping Stones blocks
- 6 strips, 4" x 42", for Stepping Stones blocks
- 4 squares, 2" x 2", for corner squares in inner border

From the assorted light blue prints, cut:
- 2 strips, 2½" x 42", for Town Square blocks

From the assorted medium blue prints, cut:
- 8 strips, 2½" x 42", for Town Square blocks

From the assorted dark blue prints, cut:
- 16 strips, 2½" x 42", for Town Square blocks

From the assorted dark red prints for Stepping Stones blocks, cut:
- 16 strips, 2¼" x 42"

From the dark red print for inner border and corner squares in outer border, cut:
- 8 strips, 2" x 42", for inner border
- 4 squares, 5" x 5", for corner squares in outer border

From the assorted red plaids, cut:
- 3 strips, 3½" x 42", for Stepping Stones blocks

From the red plaid for outer border, cut:
- 8 strips, 5" x 42"

Making the Town Square Blocks

1. Sew 4½"-wide off-white background strips to opposite sides of a 2½"-wide dark blue strip as shown to make strip set A. Make 4 strip sets. Crosscut the strip sets into 62 segments, 2½" wide.

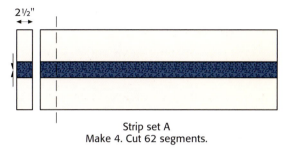

Strip set A
Make 4. Cut 62 segments.

2. Sew the 2½"-wide strips of off-white, dark blue, and medium blue together as shown to make strip set B. Make 4 strip sets. Crosscut the strip sets into 62 segments, 2½" wide.

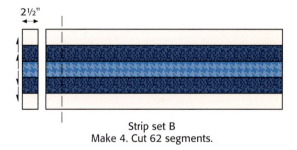

Strip set B
Make 4. Cut 62 segments.

3. Sew the 2½"-wide strips of dark blue, medium blue, and light blue together as shown to make strip set C. Make 2 strip sets. Crosscut the strip sets into 31 segments, 2½" wide.

Strip set C
Make 2. Cut 31 segments.

4. Assemble the segments as shown to make a Town Square block. Make 31 blocks.

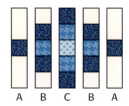

A   B   C   B   A

Make 31.

Making the Stepping Stones Blocks

1. Sew a 2¼"-wide dark red strip to opposite sides of a 7"-wide off-white strip as shown to make strip set D. Make 4 strip sets. Crosscut the strip sets into 64 segments, 2¼" wide.

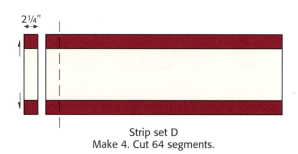

2¼"

Strip set D
Make 4. Cut 64 segments.

2. Sew 2¼"-wide off-white and dark red strips to opposite sides of a 3½"-wide off-white strip as shown to make strip unit E. Make 4 strip units. Crosscut the strip sets into 64 segments, 2¼" wide.

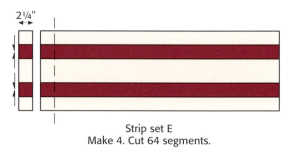

2¼"

Strip set E
Make 4. Cut 64 segments.

3. Sew a 4"-wide off-white strip to opposite sides of a 3½"-wide red plaid strip as shown to make strip set F. Make 3 strip sets. Crosscut the strip sets into 32 segments, 3½" wide.

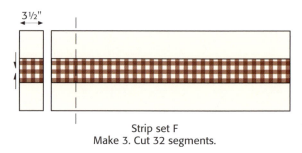

3½"

Strip set F
Make 3. Cut 32 segments.

4. Assemble the segments as shown to make a Stepping Stones block. Make 32 blocks.

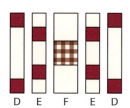

D   E   F   E   D

Make 32.

Assembling the Quilt Top

1. Referring to the quilt diagram below and the color photo on page 35, arrange the blocks in 9 horizontal rows of 7 blocks each.

2. Referring to "Making Straight-Set Quilts" on page 15, pin and sew the blocks together into rows. Carefully pin and sew the rows together, matching the seams.

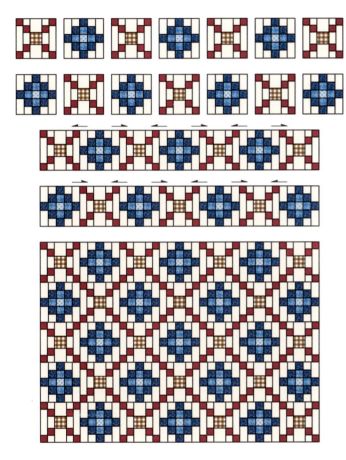

3. Referring to "Joining Border Strips" on page 17, sew the 2"-wide inner border strips end to end. Referring to "Straight-Sewn Borders with Corner Squares" on page 18, measure the quilt, trim, and sew the inner border strips to the quilt top, adding a 2" corner square to each end of the top and bottom borders.

4. Repeat step 3 with the 5"-wide outer border strips, adding a 5" corner square to each end of the top and bottom borders.

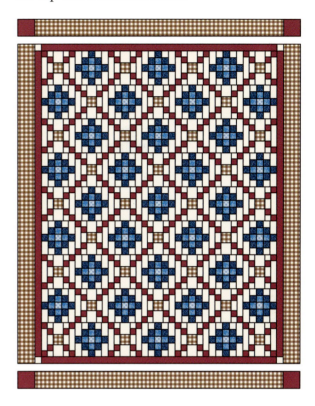

Finishing the Quilt

1. Layer the quilt top, batting, and backing; baste. Quilt as desired.

2. Trim the batting and backing even with the edges of the quilt top. Sew the binding to the edges of the quilt.

3. Make and attach a label to your finished quilt.

Kristen's Four Patch

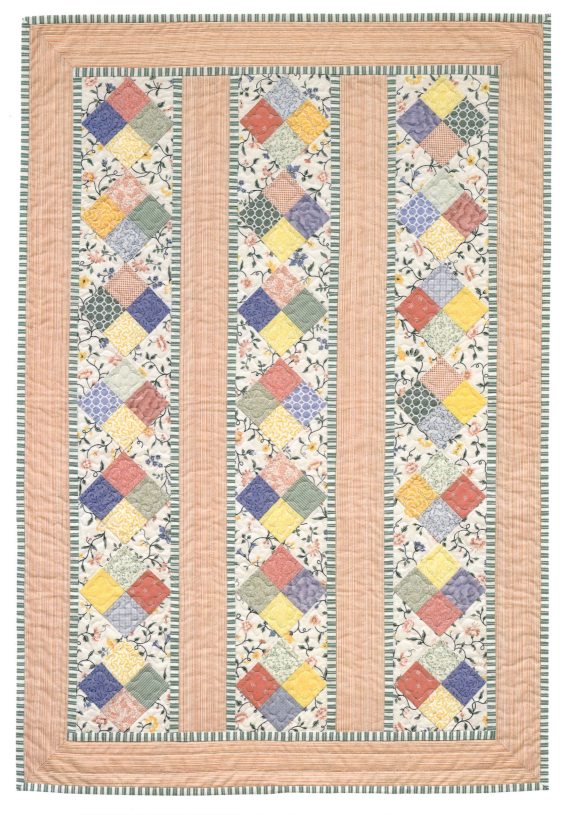

KRISTEN'S FOUR PATCH by Joan Hanson, Seattle, Washington, 1996.

From the collection of Kristen Wrigley.

When my nieces and nephew started having babies about six years ago, I started making each of them a quilt. As of this writing, I have made six quilts for their kids. There was only one girl in that bunch, and this quilt was made for her. A word to the wise: once you make the first baby a quilt, you have pretty much committed yourself to make each of them a quilt, and I don't know if I am done yet! Several other baby quilts that I made for this brood also appear in this book. This quilt consists of three rows of very easy Four Patch blocks set on-point. The color palette for the blocks was based on the viney floral print used in the side triangles. The narrow striped border adds a lot of punch to this quilt. When you are fabric shopping, keep your eye peeled for these striped fabrics and viney florals. Both can add a special zip to your quilts. —JH

FINISHED QUILT SIZE: 32½" x 47"
FINISHED BLOCK SIZE: 4"

Four Patch block

Materials 42"-wide fabric

* ¼ yd. *total* assorted blue prints for Four Patch blocks
* ¼ yd. *total* assorted red prints for Four Patch blocks
* ¼ yd. *total* assorted green prints for Four Patch blocks
* ¼ yd. *total* assorted yellow prints for Four Patch blocks
* ⅔ yd. viney floral print for side and corner triangles
* ⅝ yd. green-and-white stripe for vertical sashing, inner border, and binding
* 1½ yds. pink pinstripe for vertical sashing and outer border (cut on lengthwise grain)
* 1½ yds. for backing
* 37" x 52" piece of batting

Cutting

ALL MEASUREMENTS include ¼"-wide seam allowances.

From the assorted blue prints, cut:
* 21 squares, 2½" x 2½"

From the assorted red prints, cut:
* 21 squares, 2½" x 2½"

From the assorted green prints, cut:
* 21 squares, 2½" x 2½"

From the assorted yellow prints, cut:
* 21 squares, 2½" x 2½"

From the viney floral print, cut:
* 9 squares, 7" x 7"; cut squares twice diagonally to make 36 triangles
* 6 squares, 3¾" x 3¾"; cut squares once diagonally to make 12 triangles

From the green-and-white stripe fabric, cut:
* 8 strips, 1" x 42", for vertical sashing and inner borders
* 5 strips, 2" x 42", for binding

From the pink pinstripe fabric, cut from the lengthwise grain:
* 2 strips, 3½" x 42", for vertical sashing
* 2 strips, 3½" x 50", for outer side borders
* 2 strips, 3½" x 35", for outer top and bottom borders

Making the Blocks

ASSEMBLE 2½" blue, red, green, and yellow print squares as shown to make a Four Patch block. Make 21 blocks.

Make 21.

Assembling the Quilt Top

1. Referring to the diagram, arrange 7 Four Patch blocks and 12 side setting triangles into diagonal rows. Pin and sew the blocks and triangles together, then sew the diagonal rows together to make one long vertical row. Sew a corner setting triangle to each corner to complete the vertical row. Make 3 rows.

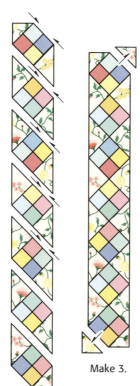

Make 3.

2. Sew a 1" x 42" green-and-white strip to opposite sides of a 3½" x 42" pink strip as shown to make a sashing strip. Make 2.

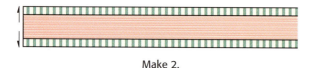

Make 2.

3. Arrange the vertical rows and the sashing strips made in step 2 as shown. Aligning the tops of the rows, pin and sew the rows together. Trim the sashing strips even with the rows of blocks.

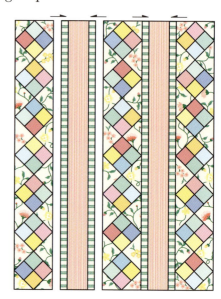

4. Referring to "Straight-Sewn Borders" on page 17, measure the quilt, trim, and sew the 1"-wide inner border strips to the quilt top.

5. Referring to "Borders with Mitered Corners" on pages 18–19, measure the quilt, trim, and sew the 3½"-wide outer border strips to the quilt top. Miter the corners.

Finishing the Quilt

1. Layer the quilt top, batting, and backing; baste. Quilt as desired.

2. Trim the batting and backing even with the edges of the quilt top. Sew the binding to the quilt.

3. Make and attach a label to your finished quilt.

Kids in the Corner

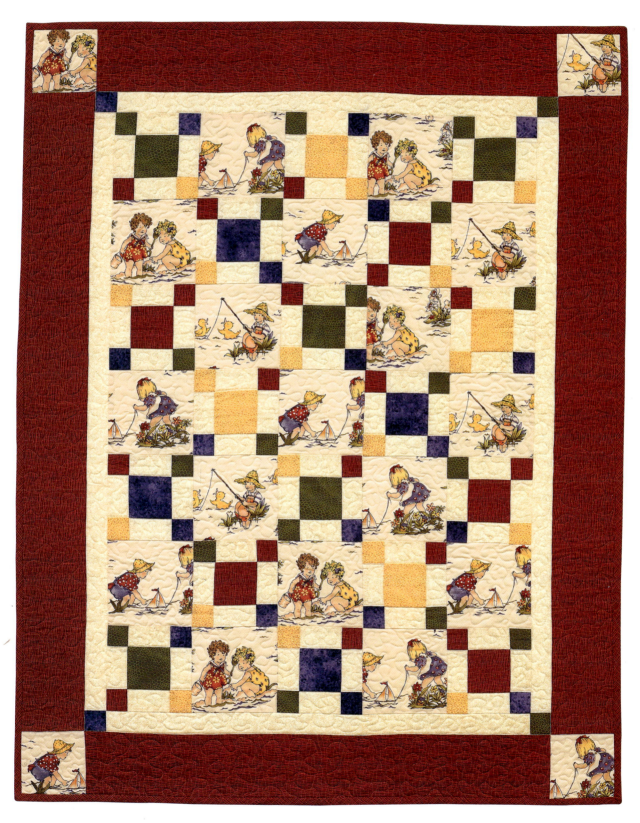

KIDS IN THE CORNER by Joan Hanson, Seattle, Washington, 1998.

From the collection of Travis Wrigley.

For those of us who love fabric and making quilts, news of a new baby automatically brings to mind plans for making a baby quilt. I made this quilt for Travis, the son of one of my nieces. We always keep our eyes open for juvenile prints that can be used for a cute, yet quick baby quilt. This quilt is a great example of letting the charming kids'-print fabric carry a quilt. One trick to using a novelty print, such as the charming kids-at-the-beach fabric, is choosing a quilt design that has spaces big enough for the print to show, yet enough design to make the quilt interesting. I chose a simple Puss in the Corner block to alternate with the kids' fabric. The 5" block size gave enough space to showcase the kids' fabric and a good size for the pieced block. Because of the spacing of the kids on the fabric, I "fussy cut" the kids'-fabric squares so that they would be centered in the blocks. You may not need to do this if the motifs on your print are closer together. —JH

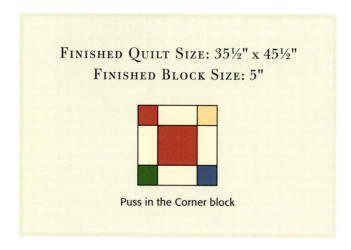

FINISHED QUILT SIZE: 35½" x 45½"
FINISHED BLOCK SIZE: 5"

Puss in the Corner block

Materials 42"-wide fabric

* ¾ yd. juvenile children's print (1 to 1½ yds. if "fussy cutting")
* ¾ yd. off-white print for Puss in the Corner blocks and inner border
* ¼ yd. each of 4 colored prints to coordinate with juvenile children's print (red, green, purple, and yellow for our print)
* 1 yd. red print for outer border and binding
* 1½ yds. for backing
* 40" x 50" piece of batting

Cutting

ALL MEASUREMENTS include ¼"-wide seam allowances.

From the juvenile children's print, cut:
* 17 squares, 5½" x 5½", for plain squares
* 4 squares, 4¼" x 4¼", for corner squares in outer border

From the off-white print, cut:
* 2 strips, 3" x 42", for Puss in the Corner blocks
* 4 strips, 1¾" x 42"; cut strips in half to make 8 strips 21" long for Puss in the Corner blocks
* 4 strips, 1¾" x 42", for inner border

From each of the 4 colored prints, cut:
* 1 strip, 1¾" x 42", for Puss in the Corner blocks (4 strips total)
* 1 strip, 3" x 21", for Puss in the Corner blocks (4 strips total)
* 1 square, 1¾" x 1¾", for corner squares in inner border (4 squares total)

From the red print, cut:
* 4 strips, 4¼" x 42", for outer border

Making the Blocks

1. Sew a 1¾" x 42" colored strip to opposite sides of a 3" x 42" off-white strip as shown to make a strip set. Repeat with the remaining 42"-long colored strips and off-white strips. Crosscut the strip sets into 36 segments, 1¾" wide.

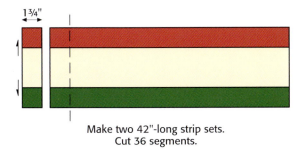

Make two 42"-long strip sets.
Cut 36 segments.

2. Sew a 1¾" x 21" off-white strip to opposite sides of a 3" x 21" colored strip as shown to make a strip set. Repeat to make 3 more strip sets, using the remaining 21"-long colored strips and background strips. Crosscut the strip sets into 18 segments, 3" wide.

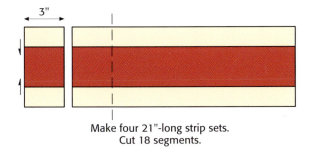

Make four 21"-long strip sets.
Cut 18 segments.

3. Assemble the segments as shown to make a Puss in the Corner block. Make 18 blocks.

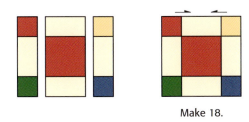

Make 18.

Assembling the Quilt Top

1. Referring to the diagram below, arrange the blocks in 7 horizontal rows of 5 blocks each.

2. Referring to "Making Straight-Set Quilts" on page 15, pin and sew the blocks together in horizontal rows. Carefully pin and sew the rows together, matching the seams.

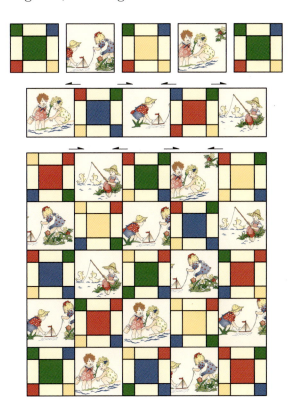

3. Referring to "Straight-Sewn Borders with Corner Squares" on page 18, measure the quilt, trim, and sew the 1¾"-wide inner border strips to the quilt top, adding a 1¾" colored square to each end of the top and bottom borders.

4. Repeat step 3 with the 4¼"-wide outer border strips, adding a 4¼" corner square to each end of the top and bottom borders.

Finishing the Quilt

1. Layer the quilt top, batting, and backing; baste. Quilt as desired.

2. Trim the batting and backing even with the edges of the quilt top. Sew the binding to the edges of the quilt.

3. Make and attach a label to your finished quilt.

Mark's Nine Patch

MARK'S NINE PATCH by the members of Needle & I, Seattle, Washington, 1991.

My son Mark received this charming quilt as a baby gift from a delightful quilt group called Needle & I. Members of the group made the little Nine Patch blocks with a wide assortment of cute animal prints. It was even hand quilted with letters, numbers, and ladybugs. We used to sit on his bed together, snuggled under this quilt, and look at all the different fabrics. He still uses it on his bed, even as a teenager.

Rotary cutting and strip piecing make this quilt a very easy project, in spite of the staggering number of little squares. As you cut strips for other projects, cut the leftover strips into 1½"-wide strips and save them for this scrappy quilt. You can also make a smaller version for a crib-sized quilt. Just remember to use an odd number of blocks in each row so that the Nine Patch blocks will end up in the corners. —JH

FINISHED QUILT SIZE: 57" x 63"
FINISHED BLOCK SIZE: 3"

Nine Patch block

Materials 42"-wide fabric

* 2¾ yds. off-white solid
* 1½ yds. *total* assorted prints
* 2 yds. red solid for border and binding (cut along lengthwise grain)
* 3½ yds. for backing
* 61" x 67" piece of batting

Cutting

ALL MEASUREMENTS include ¼"-wide seam allowances.

From the off-white solid, cut:
* 16 strips, 3½" x 42"; crosscut strips into 161 squares, 3½" x 3½"
* 27 strips, 1½" x 42", for Nine Patch blocks

From the assorted prints, cut a total of:
* 33 strips, 1½" x 42"

From the red solid, cut along the lengthwise grain:
* 2 strips, 3¼" x 60", for side borders
* 2 strips, 3¼" x 65", for top and bottom borders

Making the Blocks

1. Sew a 1½" x 42" print strip to opposite sides of a 1½" x 42" off-white strip as shown to make a strip set. Make 13 strip sets. Crosscut the strip sets into 324 segments, 1½" wide.

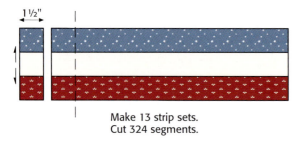

Make 13 strip sets.
Cut 324 segments.

NOTE: *For a scrappier look, cut the strips in half (1½" x 21" strips) and mix up the colors as you stitch them into strip sets. Make 25 strip sets, 21" long.*

2. Sew a 1½" x 42" off-white strip to opposite sides of a 1½" x 42" print strip as shown to make a strip set. Make 7 strip sets. Crosscut the strip sets into 162 segments, 1½" wide.

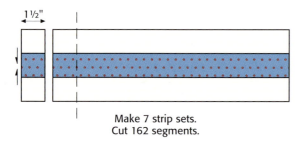

Make 7 strip sets.
Cut 162 segments.

3. Assemble the segments as shown to make a Nine Patch block. Make 162 blocks.

Make 162.

Assembling the Quilt Top

1. Referring to the diagram below, arrange the blocks in 19 horizontal rows of 17 blocks each.

2. Referring to "Making Straight-Set Quilts" on page 15, pin and sew the blocks together into rows. Carefully pin and sew the rows together, matching the seams.

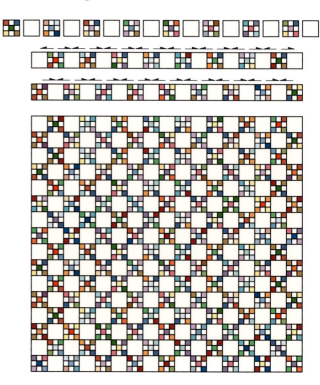

3. Referring to "Straight-Sewn Borders" on page 17, measure the quilt, trim, and sew the 3¼"-wide border strips to the quilt top.

Finishing the Quilt

1. Layer the quilt top, batting, and backing; baste. Quilt as desired.

2. Trim the batting and backing even with the edges of the quilt top. Sew the binding to the edges of the quilt.

3. Make and attach a label to your finished quilt.

Woven Ribbons

WOVEN RIBBONS by Mary Hickey, Seattle, Washington, 1998.

Machine quilted by Frankie Schmitt.

Many of us love making quilts that include the illusion of weaving as well as the feeling of depth. This little quilt offers both impressions and in a very easy format. If you think of the floral squares of fabric as a background block, the bands of three colors as the main block, and the squares of the lightest colors as the foreground block, you can quickly see how easy this quilt is.

In this quilt, a simplification of a well-known quilt designed by Miriam Nathan Roberts, the darkest reds meet the lightest greens and trick your eye into seeing the greens pass over the reds. The rosy reds and deep greens in the floral fabric simplify the choices for the colors of the woven ribbon. The design requires only four shades of each color sewn in graded order to create the enchanting illusion of elegant bands of satin ribbon woven over a chintz garden. —MH

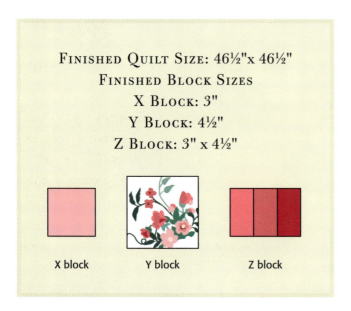

FINISHED QUILT SIZE: 46½"x 46½"
FINISHED BLOCK SIZES
X BLOCK: 3"
Y BLOCK: 4½"
Z BLOCK: 3" x 4½"

X block   Y block   Z block

Materials 42"-wide fabric

* ¼ yd. pale red solid for X blocks
* ¼ yd. pale green solid for X blocks
* 1¼ yds. floral print for Y blocks, setting pieces, and middle border
* ¼ yd. each of 3 shades (light, medium, and dark) of red solid for Z blocks
* ¼ yd. each of 3 shades (light, medium, and dark) of green solid for Z blocks
* ¾ yd. dark green solid for inner and outer borders
* 2⅞ yds. for backing
* 50" x 50" piece of batting
* ½ yd. for binding

Cutting

ALL MEASUREMENTS include ¼"-wide seam allowances.

From the pale red solid, cut:
* 2 strips, 3½" x 42"; crosscut strips into 12 squares, 3½" x 3½", for X blocks

From the pale green solid, cut:
* 2 strips, 3½" x 42"; crosscut strips into 12 squares, 3½" x 3½", for X blocks

From the floral print, cut:
* 2 strips, 4½" x 42; crosscut strips into 13 squares, 5" x 5", for Y blocks
* 5 strips, 3½" x 42", for middle border
* 2 squares, 13" x 13"; cut squares twice diagonally to make 8 side setting triangles
* 2 squares, 9" x 9"; cut squares once diagonally to make 4 corner setting triangles

From each of the 3 shades of red solid, cut:
* 2 strips, 2" x 42", for Z blocks (6 strips total)

From each of the 3 shades of green solid, cut:
* 2 strips, 2" x 42", for Z blocks (6 strips total)

From the dark green solid, cut
* 10 strips, 2" x 42", for inner and outer borders

Making the Z Blocks

1. Sew the 2"-wide light, medium, and dark strips of red together as shown to make a strip set. Make 2 strip sets. Crosscut the strip sets into 18 segments, 3½" wide.

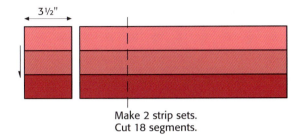

Make 2 strip sets.
Cut 18 segments.

2. Repeat step 1 with the 2"-wide light, medium, and dark strips of green.

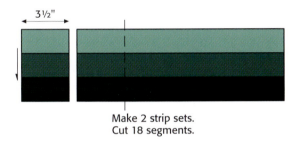

Make 2 strip sets.
Cut 18 segments.

Assembling the Quilt Top

1. Referring to the diagram above right, arrange the small squares, large squares, and pieced segments. Notice that the darkest strips of one color are always next to the lightest of the other color. Add the corner and side triangles to your arrangement.

2. Sew the units together in diagonal rows. Carefully pin and sew the rows together, adding the side triangles to the ends as shown. Sew the rows together, adding the corner triangles last.

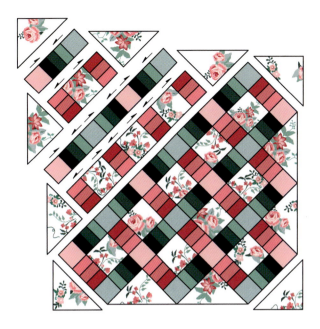

3. Using a long ruler, trim all the sides ¼" from the block points.

4. Referring to "Joining Border Strips" on page 17, sew the border strips end to end as needed. Referring to "Borders with Mitered Corners" on pages 18–19, sew the 2"-wide inner and outer border strips to opposite sides of a 3½"-wide middle border strip. Make 4 border units. Sew the border units to the quilt top. Miter the corners.

Make 4.

Finishing the Quilt

1. Layer the quilt top, batting, and backing; baste. Quilt as desired.

2. Trim the batting and backing even with the edges of the quilt top. Sew the binding to the quilt.

3. Make and attach a label to your finished quilt.

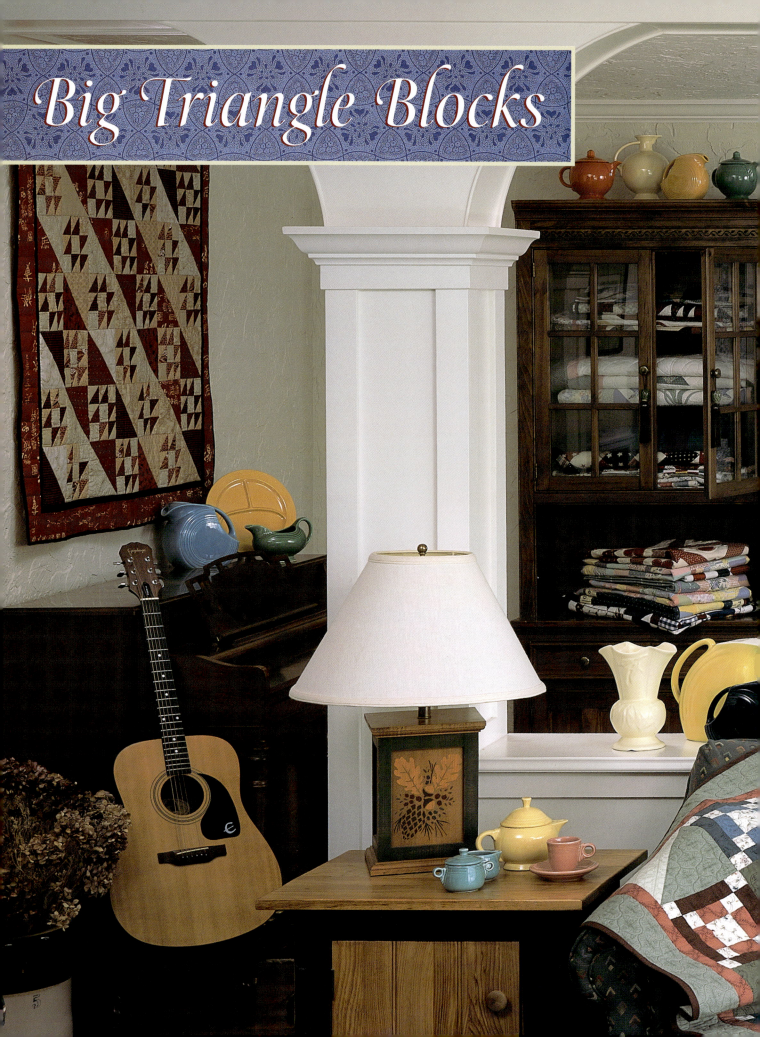

Big Triangle Blocks

Scottish Chain

SCOTTISH CHAIN by Joan Hanson, Seattle, Washington, 1999.

One of my regrets in life is not having the opportunity to know my Scottish great-grandmother, Mary Orr Whitelaw. Her husband died in the 1890s, leaving her to care for five young sons. She supported her family as a dressmaker, making fancy dresses popular in the Victorian era. She started working in her home in Edinburgh, sewing late at night and early in the morning. Eventually, she had a workshop and showroom and employed over a dozen women. One of her sons recalled that the boys always had chores to do around the shop. The one they disliked the most was sweeping up at the end of the day and picking up all the pins on the floor.

This quilt is a second cousin to an Irish Chain design; however, I call this a Scottish Chain in honor of this industrious woman. If we could have met, I know we would have hit it off. In this version, the "chain" blocks dance from corner to corner, and the three simple setting blocks with gradually shaded colors create the impression of one layer floating on another. —JH

FINISHED QUILT SIZE: 48½" x 48½"
FINISHED BLOCK SIZE: 7½"

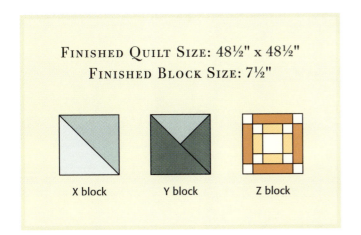

X block   Y block   Z block

Materials 42"-wide fabric

* ⅓ yd. light green print for center square and X blocks
* ⅝ yd. medium green print #1 for X and Y blocks
* ⅝ yd. dark green print for X and Y blocks
* ⅜ yd. light floral print for Z blocks
* ¼ yd. dark red print for Z blocks and inner border corner squares
* ¼ yd. dark blue print for Z blocks
* ⅛ yd. dark tan print for Z blocks
* ⅛ yd. dark yellow print for Z blocks
* ⅛ yd. medium red print #1 for Z blocks
* ⅛ yd. medium blue print for Z blocks
* ⅛ yd. medium tan print for Z blocks
* ⅛ yd. medium yellow print for Z blocks
* ⅓ yd. medium red print #2 for inner border
* ⅔ yd. medium green print #2 for outer border
* 3 yds. for backing
* 53" x 53" piece of batting
* ⅝ yd. for binding

Cutting

ALL MEASUREMENTS include ¼"-wide seam allowances.

Fabric	No. of Strips	Strip Width	No. of Pieces	Piece Size	Block or Position
Light green	1	8⅜"	2	8⅜" x 8⅜" ◹	X
			1	8" x 8"	center square
Medium green #1	1	8⅜"	4	8⅜" x 8⅜" ◹	X
	1	8¾"	1	8¾" x 8¾" ⊠	Y
Dark green	1	8⅜"	4	8⅜" x 8⅜" ◹	X and Y
	1	8¾"	1	8¾" x 8¾" ⊠	Y
			4	4½" x 4½"	corner squares
Light floral	1	3"	12	3" x 3"	Z
	4	1¾"	96	1¾" x 1¾"	Z
Dark red	3	1¾"	16	1¾" x 5½"	Z
			4	1¾" x 1¾"	corner squares
Dark blue	3	1¾"	16	1¾" x 5½"	Z
Dark tan	2	1¾"	8	1¾" x 5½"	Z
Dark yellow	2	1¾"	8	1¾" x 5½"	Z
Medium red #1	2	1¾"	16	1¾" x 3"	Z
Medium blue	2	1¾"	16	1¾" x 3"	Z
Medium tan	1	1¾"	8	1¾" x 3"	Z
Medium yellow	1	1¾"	8	1¾" x 3"	Z
Medium red #2	4	1¾"			inner border
Medium green #2	4	4½"			outer border

◹ = *Cut squares once diagonally.*
⊠ = *Cut squares twice diagonally.*

Making the X Blocks

SEW A large light green triangle to a large medium green triangle on the long side of the triangles as shown. Make 4 blocks. Sew a large medium green triangle to a large dark green triangle on the long side of the triangles as shown. Make 4 blocks.

Make 4.

Make 4.

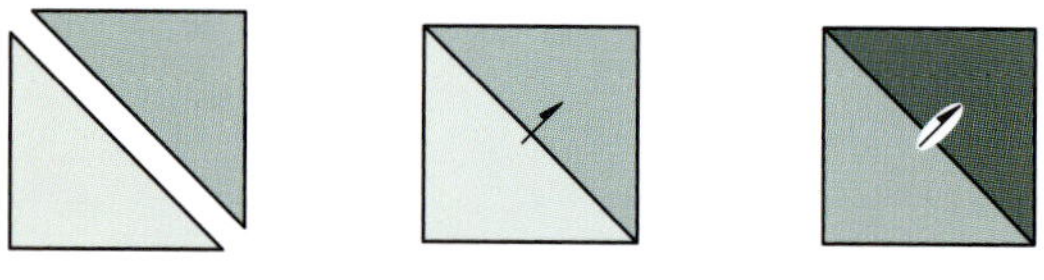

Making the Y Blocks

SEW A small medium green triangle to a small dark green triangle on the short side of the triangle as shown. Sew a large dark green triangle to the unit just made, along the long side of the triangles. Make 4 blocks.

Make 4.

Making the Z Blocks

1. For each block, assemble 4 light floral 1¾" squares, 1 light floral 3" square, and 4 medium-colored 3"-long rectangles as shown. Keeping in the same color family, add a dark-colored 5½"-long rectangle to the top and bottom of the unit.

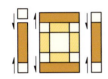

2. Sew a 1¾" light floral square to each end of a dark-colored 5½"-long rectangle as shown. Make 2 for each block. Sew these to a center unit made in step 1, keeping the color families the same. Make 4 blue blocks, 4 red blocks, 2 yellow blocks, and 2 tan blocks.

Make 4 blue blocks, 4 red blocks, 2 yellow blocks, and 2 tan blocks.

Assembling the Quilt Top

1. Referring to the diagram above right, arrange the blocks in 5 horizontal rows of 5 blocks each.

2. Referring to "Making Straight-Set Quilts" on page 15, pin and sew the blocks together in horizontal rows. Carefully pin and sew the rows together, matching the seams.

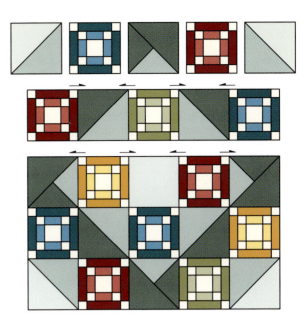

3. Referring to "Straight-Sewn Borders with Corner Squares" on page 18, measure the quilt, trim, and sew the 1¾"-wide inner border strips to the quilt top, adding a 1¾" corner square to each end of the top and bottom borders.

4. Repeat step 3 with the 4½"-wide outer border strips, adding a 4½" corner square to each end of the top and bottom borders.

Finishing the Quilt

1. Layer the quilt top, batting, and backing; baste. Quilt as desired.

2. Trim the batting and backing even with the edges of the quilt top. Sew the binding to the edges of the quilt.

3. Make and attach a label to your finished quilt.

The Permanent Incomplete

THE PERMANENT INCOMPLETE by Mary Hickey, Seattle, Washington, 2000.

Machine quilted by Frankie Schmitt.

My oldest daughter, Maureen, went to Wisconsin last summer to study advanced Thai language as part of her graduate studies. Shortly after arriving in Wisconsin, she received an invitation to visit Seoul, South Korea, to read a paper at a conference of geographers. The Korean invitation included airfare and expenses but required her to leave Wisconsin two days before the end of her Thai program. She went to see her Thai professor and explained the problem. She asked if she could take the final exam early or if she could write an extra paper to make up for the missed work. The professor was indignant and quite adamant that Maureen must not miss the last two days of summer classes. He could not possibly allow her to miss two days, and if Maureen did miss the days she would receive a "permanent incomplete." A permanent incomplete would go on Maureen's record and could never be changed. Maureen thought over this dreadful announcement and said calmly, "A permanent incomplete if I miss two days? Well, in that case, I think I'll leave five days early."

Asian in character and upbeat in temperament, the pictured quilt commemorates this funny family story and creates a dramatic statement without any tricky sewing. Start by finding a bold fabric to use as the outer border and for some of the large and small triangles in the blocks. Add a slim band of black to spice up the final product. The pictured quilt is missing one small triangle and now creates a stunning focal point in an academic office. —MH

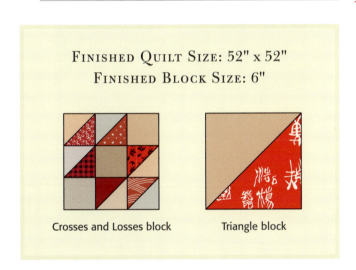

Finished Quilt Size: 52" x 52"
Finished Block Size: 6"

Crosses and Losses block   Triangle block

Materials 42"-wide fabric

* 1⅛ yds. red print #1 for small and large triangles and outer border
* ½ yd. each of 6 assorted red prints for small and large triangles
* ½ yd. each of 7 assorted tan prints for small and large triangles
* ¼ yd. black solid for inner border
* 3¼ yds. for backing
* 56" x 56" piece of batting
* ⅝ yd. for binding

Cutting

ALL MEASUREMENTS include ¼"-wide seam allowances.

From red print #1, cut:
* 1 square, 12" x 12", for half-square triangles
* 3 squares, 7" x 7"; cut squares once diagonally to make 6 large triangles
* 5 strips, 4¼" x 42", for outer borders

From the 6 assorted red prints, cut a total of:
* 6 squares, 12" x 12", for half-square triangles
* 10 squares, 7" x 7"; cut squares once diagonally to make 19 large triangles

From the 7 assorted tan prints, cut a total of:
* 7 squares, 12" x 12", for half-square triangles
* 13 squares, 7" x 7"; cut squares once diagonally to make 25 large triangles

From the black solid, cut:
* 5 strips, 1½" x 42", for inner borders

Making the Crosses and Losses Blocks

1. Referring to "Making Half-Square Triangle Units" on pages 12–14, use the 12" squares of red and tan to make 144 red-and-tan half-square triangle units.

> Cut the bias strips 2½" wide.
> Cut the segments 2½" wide.
> Cut the squares 2½" x 2½".

Make 144.

2. Assemble 6 triangle units and 3 squares as shown to make a Crosses and Losses block. Make 24 blocks.

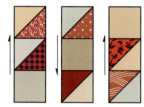 

Make 24.

Making the Triangle Blocks

Sew a large tan triangle to a large red triangle as shown to make a triangle block. Make 25 blocks.

Make 25.

Assembling the Quilt Top

1. Referring to the diagram below, arrange the blocks in 7 horizontal rows of 7 blocks each.

2. Referring to "Making Straight-Set Quilts" on page 15, pin and sew the blocks together in horizontal rows. Carefully pin and sew the rows together, matching the seams.

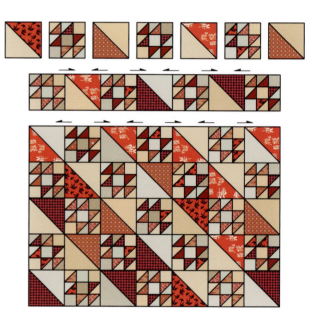

3. Referring to "Joining Border Strips" on page 17, sew the border strips end to end. Referring to "Borders with Mitered Corners" on pages 18–19, sew the inner and outer border strips together. Make 4 border units. Sew the border units to the quilt top. Miter the corners.

Finishing the Quilt

1. Layer the quilt top, batting, and backing; baste. Quilt as desired.

2. Trim the batting and backing even with the edges of the quilt top. Sew the binding to the edges of the quilt.

3. Make and attach a label to your finished quilt.

Sheriff's Log Cabin

SHERIFF'S LOG CABIN by Mary Hickey, Seattle, Washington, 2000.

Machine quilted by Frankie Schmitt.

Twice a year, our large quilt group gathers at a camp in the foothills of the Cascade Mountains for a three-day retreat. I am always careful to take a project that I have made all the decisions about. I find it very nerve-racking to have too much help with design and color choices. Not only do people make suggestions, but they expect you to follow them. I had great fun planning the design and choosing the colors for this quilt. I knew I wanted to use the sunny butternut yellow and the blues and whites. A Log Cabin—this would be so simple to make at the retreat—just sew the strips together. . . .

Toward the end of the first day, my friend Ann commented that I seemed to be whining more than usual. Yes, it was very tedious. Ann suggested that I make an alternate block. I thought this was a ridiculous idea, but I had to be polite, so why not give it a try? I decided to use some really big triangles as an alternate block. The triangles covered a lot of territory for a very small amount of work, and to my surprise, they really looked great. Presto! The quilt zoomed along after that. I resumed stitching logs, made the alternate blocks, and thought I was finished with the blocks.

Then, another friend suggested ever so tactfully that perhaps the quilt would be a bit more interesting if I added something like a heart to the dark blue triangles. Hmmm, this would be entirely too much trouble, but I had to admit, those blue triangles were big and flat. And, I had to be polite. I drew a slightly chubby star, but I did not want to hand or machine appliqué stars or fuse them. I devised a super-simple system for sewing the stars. Try the "Face-and-Turn Appliqué" method for creating handsome finished appliqué stars in the blink of an eye. —MH

FINISHED QUILT SIZE: 92½" x 92½"
FINISHED BLOCK SIZE: 10"

Log Cabin block   Triangle block

Materials 42"-wide fabric

* 1¼ yds. yellow print #1 for block centers and stars
* ⅓ yd. each of 12 assorted light blue prints for blocks
* ⅓ yd. each of 12 assorted dark blue prints for blocks
* 1 yd. white fabric for lining stars
* 1 yd. yellow print #2 for inner border
* 1¼ yds. dark blue print for outer border
* 8¼ yds. for backing
* 97" x 97" piece of batting
* 1 yd. for binding

Cutting

ALL MEASUREMENTS include ¼"-wide seam allowances.

From yellow print #1, cut:
- 3 strips, 3" x 42"; cut strips in half to make 6 strips, 3" x 21", for Log Cabin block centers
- 5 strips, 6" x 42"; crosscut strips into 32 squares, 6" x 6", for appliqué stars

From the assorted light blue prints, cut a total of:
- 16 squares, 11" x 11"; cut squares once diagonally to make 32 large triangles
- 32 strips, 1¾" x 42", for Log Cabin blocks; cut 6 different strips in half to make 12 strips, 1¾" x 21"

From the assorted dark blue prints, cut a total of:
- 16 squares, 11" x 11"; cut squares once diagonally to make 32 large triangles
- 42 strips, 1¾" x 42", for Log Cabin blocks

From the white fabric, cut:
- 5 strips, 6" x 42"; crosscut strips into 32 squares, 6" x 6", for appliqué stars

From yellow print #2, cut:
- 9 strips, 3" x 42", for inner border

From the dark blue print, cut:
- 9 strips, 4" x 42", for outer border

Making the Log Cabin Blocks

1. Sew a 1¾" x 21" light blue strip to a 3" x 21" yellow #1 strip. Make 6 strip sets, using a different light blue print in each one. Crosscut the strip sets into 32 segments, 3" wide.

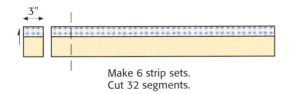

Make 6 strip sets.
Cut 32 segments.

2. Place a segment from step 1 on top of a 1¾" x 21" strip of the same light blue print, with right sides together and the light blue print facing you. Sew along the right-hand edge. Press the seam away from the center and trim the strip to the size of the segment.

3. Working in a clockwise direction with the last strip just added closest to you, sew the next 2 strips from the dark blue print in the same manner.

4. Continue to add light and dark strips until the block has 3 rows of lights and 3 rows of darks around the central yellow square. Make 32 Log Cabin blocks.

Make 32.

Making the Triangle Blocks

SEW A light triangle to a dark triangle to make a triangle block. Make 32 blocks.

Make 32.

Making the Stars

1. Prepare the stars for appliqué, referring to "Making the Hearts: Face-and-Turn Appliqué" on page 25. Use the 6" squares of white and yellow and substitute the star shape for the heart shape.

2. Pin a star to the center of each dark blue triangle. Consider making your stars from a variety of colors, or try placing the star over the seam line of the light and dark blue triangles. (Or make hearts!)

3. Use the "bar-tack" stitch on your sewing machine to tack the points and corners of each star onto your triangle blocks as shown.

Assembling the Quilt Top

1. Referring to the diagram below, arrange the blocks in 8 horizontal rows of 8 blocks each.

2. Referring to "Making Straight-Set Quilts" on page 15, pin and sew the blocks together in horizontal rows. Carefully pin and sew the rows together, matching the seams.

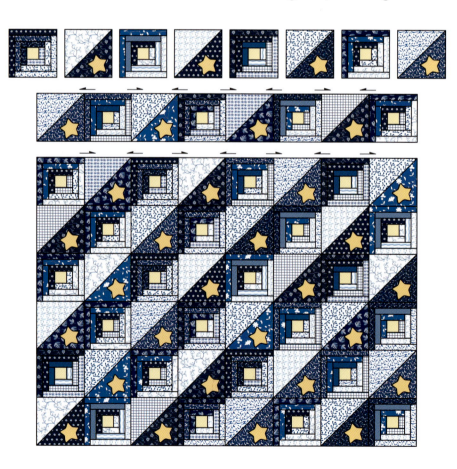

3. Referring to "Joining Border Strips" on page 17, sew the border strips end to end. Referring to "Borders with Mitered Corners" on pages 18–19, sew the inner and outer border strips together. Make 4 border units. Sew the border units to the quilt top. Miter the corners.

Finishing the Quilt

1. Layer the quilt top, batting, and backing; baste. Quilt as desired.

2. Trim the batting and backing even with the edges of the quilt top. Sew the binding to the edges of the quilt.

3. Make and attach a label to your finished quilt.

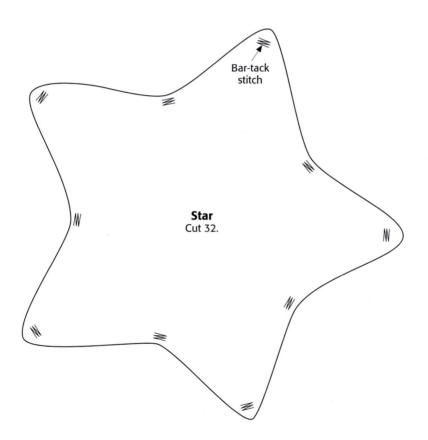

Bar-tack stitch

Star
Cut 32.

Folded-Corner Triangles

Gabriel Meets Dick and Jane

GABRIEL MEETS DICK AND JANE by Joan Hanson, Seattle, Washington, 2000.

From the collection of Gabriel Puhky.

Who can resist those charming children's prints that are always popping up in quilt shops? The challenge in using them is finding a quilt block that has a large-enough piece in which to feature the design in the fabric, while having small-enough pieces so that the quilt doesn't look clunky. The 6" Snowball block is the perfect choice for showing off the fabric design, and the alternating Nine Patch block allows for some finer piecing.

I chose three colors from the children's print to use in this quilt: cool green and blue for the Snowball blocks and the Nine Patch blocks, plus red for the Nine Patch blocks as an accent. The blues form a diagonal chain in one direction and the greens in the other. A wide border of the children's print lets more of the design show. The larger-than-crib size is the perfect size for baby to grow into and use for several years. The baby in this case is Gabriel, who took his time coming to our family. My niece, Kim, waited until after age forty to have him, and he waited an extra two weeks to arrive after we expected him. —JH

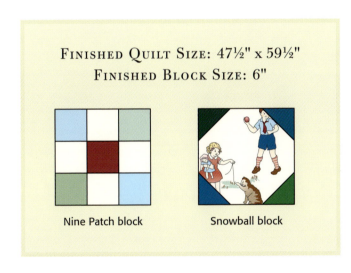

FINISHED QUILT SIZE: 47½" x 59½"
FINISHED BLOCK SIZE: 6"

Nine Patch block

Snowball block

Materials 42"-wide fabric

* 1¾ yds. children's print for Snowball blocks and middle border
* ⅓ yd. *total* assorted dark blue fabrics for Snowball blocks
* ⅓ yd. *total* assorted dark green fabrics for Snowball blocks
* ⅔ yd. muslin for Nine Patch blocks
* ⅓ yd. *total* assorted light blue fabrics for Nine Patch blocks
* ⅓ yd. *total* assorted light green fabrics for Nine Patch blocks
* ¼ yd. *total* assorted red fabrics for Nine Patch blocks
* ⅓ yd. red solid for inner border
* 1⅛ yds. dark blue solid for outer border and binding
* 3⅓ yds. for backing
* 52" x 64" piece of batting

Cutting

ALL MEASUREMENTS include ¼"-wide seam allowances.

From the children's print, cut in order (borders first):

* 2 strips, 5" x 44", along the crosswise grain for middle top and bottom borders
* 2 strips, 5" x 49", along the lengthwise grain for middle side borders
* 17 squares, 6½" x 6½", for Snowball blocks

From the assorted dark blue fabrics, cut a total of:
- 34 squares, 2½" x 2½", for Snowball blocks

From the assorted dark green fabrics, cut a total of:
- 34 squares, 2½" x 2½", for Snowball blocks

From the muslin, cut:
- 6 strips, 2½" x 42", for Nine Patch blocks

From the assorted light blue fabrics, cut:
- 3 strips, 2½" x 42", for Nine Patch blocks

From the assorted light green fabrics, cut:
- 3 strips, 2½" x 42", for Nine Patch blocks

From the assorted red fabrics, cut:
- 3 strips, 2½" x 21", for Nine Patch blocks

From the red solid, cut:
- 5 strips, 1¾" x 42", for inner border

From the dark blue solid, cut:
- 5 strips, 3¼" x 42", for outer border

Making the Nine Patch Blocks

1. Sew a 2½" x 42" light blue and light green strip to opposite sides of a 2½" x 42" muslin strip as shown to make a strip set. Make 3 strip sets. Crosscut the strip sets into 36 segments, 2½" wide.

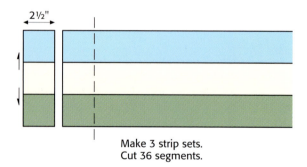

2½"

Make 3 strip sets.
Cut 36 segments.

2. Cut the remaining 2½" x 42" muslin strips in half to make 6 strips, 2½" x 21". Sew a 2½" x 21" muslin strip to each side of a 2½" x 21" red strip as shown to make a strip set. Make 3 strip sets. Crosscut the strip sets into 18 segments, 2½" wide.

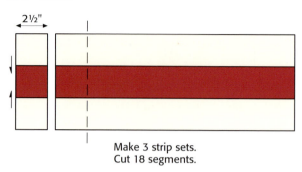

2½"

Make 3 strip sets.
Cut 18 segments.

3. Assemble the segments as shown to make a Nine Patch block. Make 18 blocks.

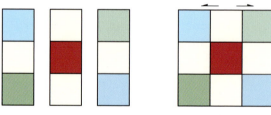

Make 18.

Making the Snowball Blocks

1. Referring to "Making Folded-Corner Triangles" on page 12, place a creased 2½" dark green square on opposite diagonal corners of a 6½" children's print square as shown. Sew along the diagonal crease and trim the excess fabric.

2. Repeat with creased 2½" dark blue squares on the remaining 2 opposite corners. Make 17 Snowball blocks.

Make 17.

Assembling the Quilt Top

1. Referring to the diagram below, arrange the blocks in 7 horizontal rows of 5 blocks each, alternating the Nine Patch blocks and Snowball blocks.

2. Referring to "Making Straight-Set Quilts" on page 15, sew the blocks together into rows. Carefully pin and sew the rows together, matching the seams.

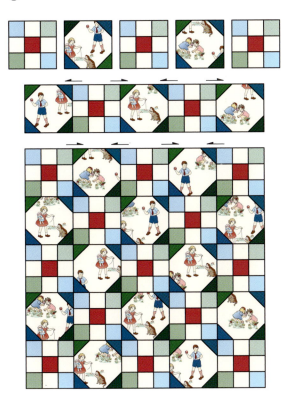

3. Referring to "Joining Border Strips" on page 17, sew the border strips end to end. Referring to "Straight-Sewn Borders" on page 17, measure the quilt, trim, and sew the 1¾"-wide inner border strips to the quilt top.

4. Measure the quilt, trim, and sew the 5"-wide middle border strips to the quilt top.

5. Repeat step 3 with the 3¼"-wide outer border strips.

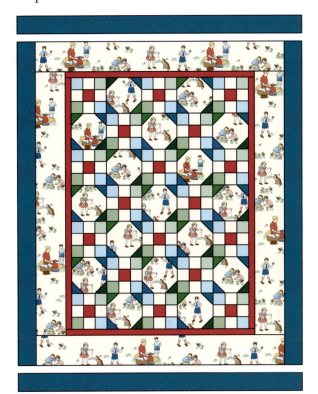

Finishing the Quilt

1. Layer the quilt top, batting, and backing; baste. Quilt as desired.

2. Trim the batting and backing even with the edges of the quilt top. Sew the binding to the edges of the quilt.

3. Make and attach a label to your finished quilt.

Friendship Stars

FRIENDSHIP STARS by Joan Hanson, Seattle, Washington, 1999.

bout ten years ago, I attended an author workshop for quilting authors from around the country at
That Patchwork Place. I felt quite honored to be included in a group of such talented and creative
women that I had admired from afar. People were passing around books and bits of fabric for each other
to sign. I decided to pass around some 3 1/2" white squares and a blue pen to collect signatures, not having a specific design in mind. I stuck them in a drawer and have pulled them out every once in a while
and thought about what I would do with them. Last year, while looking for projects to take to a quilt
retreat, I finally decided that the time had come to make them into a quilt. The white squares became
the centers of a simple Sawtooth Star block, with shades of clear pastels for the background. I used four
favorite colors—blue, green, pink, and yellow—for the background. Notice that there are nine blue
blocks, eight green blocks, seven pink blocks, and only six yellow blocks. This allows the cool, soothing
blues and greens to dominate, and the warm pinks and yellows to add the sparkle.

After completing the thirty blocks, I ran across the stripe for the sashing in my fabric collection and
knew that it would be the perfect way to set the stars together. The medium-colored corner squares in
the blocks and the darker sashing squares work together to create a secondary Nine Patch design. I was
especially pleased with the corner squares in the borders and how they draw the eye into the quilt. This
is an easy border treatment that I hope you will keep in mind for other quilts. Even though it took a
long time from start to finish, this quilt almost seemed to design itself. —JH

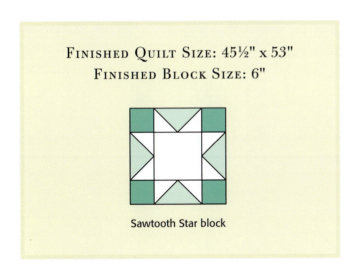

FINISHED QUILT SIZE: 45½" x 53"
FINISHED BLOCK SIZE: 6"

Sawtooth Star block

Materials 42"-wide fabric

* 1¼ yds. white solid for stars
* ¾ yd. *total* of light solids in blue, green, pink,
  and yellow for stars
* ½ yd. *total* of medium solids in blue, green,
  pink, and yellow for stars

* ¼ yd. *total* of dark solids in blue, green, pink,
  and yellow for sashing squares and pieced corner squares
* ⅞ yd. multicolored stripe for sashing
* ¾ yd. medium blue solid for border
* 2⅞ yds. for backing
* 50" x 57" piece of batting
* ½ yd. for binding

Cutting

ALL MEASUREMENTS include ¼"-wide seam
allowances.

NOTE: *Signatures in blocks make a quilt extra special and are a fun way of marking a special occasion.
To make it easier to use a pen on fabric, stabilize the
fabric by pressing a piece of freezer paper (shiny side
toward the fabric) to the wrong side of the fabric
before cutting out your squares.*

From the white solid, cut:

- 3 strips, 3½" x 42"; crosscut strips into 30 squares, 3½" x 3½", for star centers
- 12 strips, 2" x 42"; crosscut strips into 240 squares, 2" x 2", for star points

From the light blue solid, cut:

- 36 rectangles, 2" x 3½", for sides of Star blocks

From the light green solid, cut:

- 32 rectangles, 2" x 3½", for sides of Star blocks

From the light pink solid, cut:

- 28 rectangles, 2" x 3½", for sides of Star blocks

From the light yellow solid, cut:

- 24 rectangles, 2" x 3½", for sides of Star blocks

From the medium blue solid, cut:

- 36 squares, 2" x 2", for corners of Star blocks

From the medium green solid, cut:

- 32 squares, 2" x 2", for corners of Star blocks

From the medium pink solid, cut:

- 28 squares, 2" x 2", for corners of Star blocks

From the medium yellow solid, cut:

- 24 squares, 2" x 2", for corners of Star blocks

From the dark blue, green, pink, and yellow solids, cut a total of:

- 50 squares, 2" x 2", for sashing squares and pieced corner squares

From the multicolor stripe, cut:

- 12 strips, 2" x 42"; crosscut strips into 71 rectangles, 2" x 6½", for sashing strips
- 16 squares, 2" x 2", for pieced corner squares

From the medium blue solid, cut:

- 5 strips, 3½" x 42", for borders
- 8 squares, 2" x 2", for pieced border unit

Making the Blocks

1. Referring to "Making Folded-Corner Triangles" on page 12, place a creased 2" white square on opposite ends of a 2" x 3½" light rectangle as shown to make a star-point unit. Make the number of units indicated for each color.

Make 36 blue units,
32 green units,
28 pink units,
and 24 yellow units.

2. Assemble the star-point units and the 2" and 3½" squares as shown to make a Sawtooth Star block. Make 9 blue blocks, 8 green blocks, 7 pink blocks, and 6 yellow blocks.

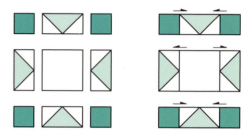

Make 9 blue blocks, 8 green blocks,
7 pink blocks, and 6 yellow blocks.

Assembling the Quilt Top

1. Arrange the blocks and sashing strips in 6 horizontal rows of 5 blocks and 6 sashing strips each. Alternate with 7 rows of 6 sashing squares and 5 sashing strips.

NOTE: *If possible, arrange the blocks, sashing strips, and setting squares on a design wall or floor. Make sure that the colors are arranged to your liking. Squint at them or look at them through a reducing glass to test the color arrangement.*

2. Referring to "Making Straight-Set Quilts" on page 15, pin and sew the units together in horizontal rows. Carefully pin the rows together, matching the seams; then join the rows and press.

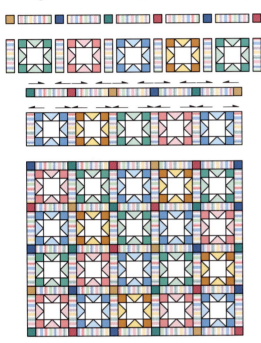

3. Sew a 2" medium blue square to a 2" striped square as shown. Make 8 units.

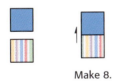

Make 8.

4. Using the remaining 2" squares, sew 2 colored and 2 striped squares together as shown to make a pieced corner square. Make 4.

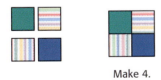

Make 4.

5. Referring to "Joining Border Strips" on page 17, sew the 3½"-wide border strips end to end as needed. Measure the length and width of the quilt, excluding the outer sashing and sashing-square rows and add ½" for seam allowances. Cut the border strips to those lengths. Add the units from step 3 to the end of each border strip as shown.

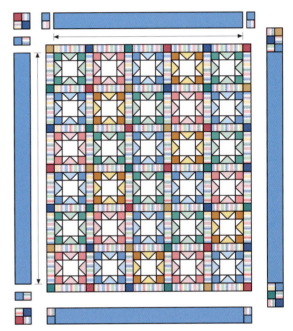

6. Pin and sew a border-strip unit to opposite sides of the quilt top. Add a pieced corner square to each end of the top and bottom border strips; add these to the top and bottom edges of the quilt top.

Finishing the Quilt

1. Layer the quilt top, batting, and backing; baste. Quilt as desired.

2. Trim the batting and backing even with the edges of the quilt top. Sew the binding to the edges of the quilt.

3. Make and attach a label to your finished quilt.

Cottage Garden

COTTAGE GARDEN by Mary Hickey, Seattle, Washington, 1997.

Machine quilted by Frankie Schmitt.

Bouquets of roses entwined with clusters of pansies peek through the pastel latticework of this romantic quilt. Quilters love to make quilts that create illusions and this is a very easy one to make. Simple X blocks combine with the faithful Snowball block to make this lovely piece of trickery. Look closely and see that the peach strips span the length of half the blocks, and green strips dominate the other half. By alternating the X blocks with the Snowball blocks, the Xs are linked in a woven pattern similar to a garden trellis.

Since all of the seams are straight seams and there are no complex triangle units to prepare in advance, this is a truly simple quilt. However, do be careful to work systematically by checking the color placement of each piece. Arrange the blocks on your design wall, and pin them together as you remove them from the wall to sew. These blocks are very sneaky and have a tendency to tip themselves over sideways when you are not looking. —MH

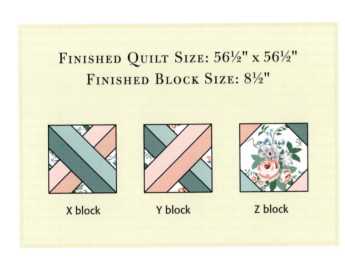

FINISHED QUILT SIZE: 56½" x 56½"
FINISHED BLOCK SIZE: 8½"

X block   Y block   Z block

Materials 42"-wide fabric

* 1½ yd. floral print #1 for Z blocks
* ⅞ yd. light peach for X, Y, and Z blocks
* ⅞ yd. medium peach for X, Y, and Z blocks
* ⅞ yd. light green for X, Y, and Z blocks
* ⅞ yd. medium green #1 for X, Y, and Z blocks
* ½ yd. medium green #2 for inner border
* 1 yd. floral print #2 for outer border
* 3½ yds. for backing
* 60" x 60" piece of batting
* ½ yd. for binding

Cutting

ALL MEASUREMENTS include ¼"-wide seam allowances.

From floral print #1, cut:
* 13 squares, 9" x 9"
* 12 squares, 4" x 4"; cut squares twice diagonally to make 48 triangles for under-trellis pieces

From each of the light and medium peach fabrics, cut:
* 1 strip, 3⅜" x 42" (2 strips total); crosscut each strip into 12 squares, 3⅜" x 3⅜", for Z blocks
* 2 strips, 12" x 42" (4 strips total), for X and Y blocks

From each of the light green and medium green #1 fabrics, cut:
* 1 strip, 3⅜" x 42" (2 strips total); crosscut each strip into 12 squares, 3⅜" x 3⅜" for Z blocks
* 2 strips, 12" x 42" (4 strips total), for X and Y blocks

From medium green #2, cut:
* 5 strips, 2½" x 42", for inner border

From floral print #2, cut:
* 6 strips, 5¼" x 42", for outer border

Making the X and Y Blocks

NOTE: *The trellis pieces that look as if they are on top are called "Over-Trellis" pieces; they look like elongated diamonds. The ones that look like they are behind are the "Under-Trellis" pieces.*

X block
"over-trellis" pieces

X block
"under-trellis" pieces

OVER-TRELLIS PIECES

1. Place a 12" x 42" light peach strip over a medium peach strip, right sides together, and cut 8 bias strips 2½" wide as shown. Layer the remaining 12" x 42" light peach and medium peach strips, and cut 4 bias strips 2½" wide. Save the ends for cutting other pieces. Repeat with the light green and medium green #1 strips.

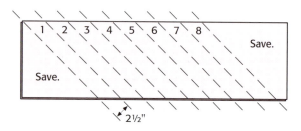

2. With right sides together, sew each pair of bias strips together along the long edges as shown. If you layered your fabrics correctly, you should be sewing a light peach strip to a medium peach strip, and a light green strip to a medium green #1 strip. Press the seams open.

3. Place the diagonal line of the Bias Square ruler on the seam line as shown and trim the point to a perfect right angle.

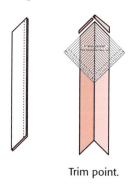

Trim point.

4. Measure from the point you have just made and make a mark 12¾" from the point as shown. Mark 6 green pairs and 6 peach pairs. Set the rest aside for "under-trellis" pieces.

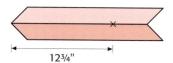

12¾"

5. Place the diagonal line of the Bias Square ruler on the seam line, and the corner of the ruler on the 12¾" mark as shown. Trim around the corner of the ruler to make a point. The piece should measure 12¾" from point to point.

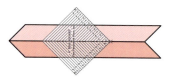

12¾"

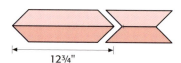

Make 6 peach and 6 green.

UNDER-TRELLIS PIECES

1. Fold the remaining bias-strip pairs in half as shown below. (Although folding the units in half may use a bit more fabric, it does ensure that you will wind up with the right color on the correct side of each pair.) Cut 2 rectangles 4⅝" wide from the folded bias-strip pair as shown.

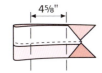

Cut 12 peach rectangles
and 12 green rectangles.

2. Place a corner of the Bias Square ruler at one end of the rectangle, and the diagonal line of the ruler on the seam line; trim around the corner of the ruler to make a point. The piece should measure 4⅝" from the point to the straight edge. Repeat for all rectangles to make the "under-trellis" pieces.

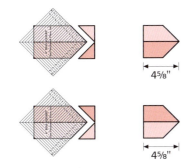

Cut 6 peach and 6 green in each orientation.

3. Sew a floral triangle to opposite sides of an under-trellis piece, lining up the bottom of the triangles with the straight edge of the piece as shown.

4. Join the over-trellis and under-trellis pieces as shown to make the X and Y blocks. Pay attention to the placement of the colors in each block. Keep each color pair pointing in the same direction and always sew the lighter colors toward the upper edge of the block.

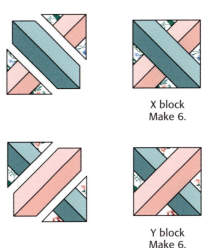

X block
Make 6.

Y block
Make 6.

Making the Z (Snowball) Blocks

1. Cut one square each, 3⅜" x 3⅜", from the light peach, medium peach, light green, and medium green #1. You should now have thirteen 3⅜" squares of each trellis color. Fold the squares in half diagonally and gently press a crease.

2. Arrange the X blocks and Y blocks on your design wall, with the colors pointing in the direction you want them to appear in the quilt. In our quilt, the peaches point to the right and the greens to the left. Alternate the 9" floral squares with the blocks. Pin a creased square of each trellis color on the corners of the squares to match the adjacent colors in the X and Y blocks.

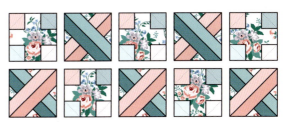

3. Referring to "Making Folded-Corner Triangles" on page 12, sew the creased squares to the large floral square. Make 13 blocks.

Stitch.   Trim.   Press.

Z block
Make 13.

Assembling the Quilt Top

1. Referring to the diagram below, arrange the blocks in 5 horizontal rows of 5 blocks each. Keep each color pointing in the same direction and the lighter colors positioned toward the top of the blocks.

2. Referring to "Making Straight-Set Quilts" on page 15, pin and sew the blocks together in horizontal rows. Carefully pin and sew the rows together, matching the seams.

3. Referring to "Joining Border Strips" on page 17, sew the 2½"-wide inner border strips end to end as needed. Referring to "Straight-Sewn Borders" on page 17, measure the quilt, trim, and sew the inner border strips to the quilt top.

4. Repeat step 3 with the 5¼"-wide outer border strips.

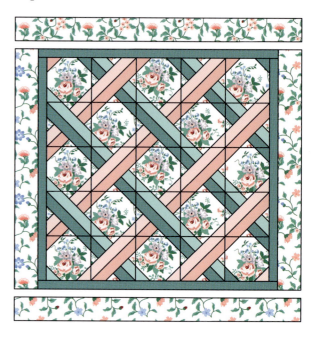

Finishing the Quilt

1. Layer the quilt top, batting, and backing; baste. Quilt as desired.

2. Trim the batting and backing even with the edges of the quilt top. Sew the binding to the edges of the quilt.

3. Make and attach a label to your finished quilt.

Star Within a Star

STAR WITHIN A STAR by Mary Hickey, Keyport, Washington, 1997.

Machine quilted by Frankie Schmitt.

This Star within a Star pattern is not only very easy to make but it also lends itself to featuring a special fabric, such as the sun-and-moon batik print here. Of course, I had to buy enough batik fabric to use in the quilt and still have a substantial piece left over. I gathered ample fabric to make several king-size quilts and began planning. I had enough pale yellow to make five or six hundred stars, so I planned for five. I could have wrapped my house in gold fabric, so I made four blocks and several half blocks. I didn't seem to have the right color plaid for the first border, so I bought four more candidates and then used the one I intended in the first place. After stitching the plaid borders, I felt I was just getting warmed up, so I decided to add the sawtooth borders. Then I decided to make just one more simple border. As you can see, I don't always plan my quilts as well as I could. However, I wanted to make a Star within a Star quilt with a masculine flavor and this fits the bill.

The subdued yellow and gold fabrics allow the sun-and-moon fabric to glow without too much visual confusion and competition. If you do not want to sew sawtooth borders, a gold-and-navy plaid border would work well to create energy without consuming so much time. —MH

FINISHED QUILT SIZE: 45" x 45"
FINISHED BLOCK SIZE: 8"

Star block   Alternate block

Materials 42"-wide fabric

* 1⅝ yds. navy blue print for background and outer border
* ¼ yd. pale yellow for Star blocks
* ⅝ yd. gold for alternate blocks
* ½ yd. yellow plaid for inner border
* 1¼ yds. navy blue solid for sawtooth border and binding
* ½ yd. each of 3 assorted yellows or golds for sawtooth border
* 2¾ yds. for backing
* 49" x 49" piece of batting

Cutting

ALL MEASUREMENTS include ¼"-wide seam allowances.

From the navy blue print, cut:

- 1 strip, 6³⁄₁₆" x 42"; crosscut strip into 4 squares, 6³⁄₁₆" x 6³⁄₁₆", for alternate blocks
- 6 strips, 4½" x 42"; crosscut strips as follows:
  - 9 squares, 4½" x 4½", for Star blocks
  - 20 rectangles, 2½" x 4½", for Star blocks
  - 12 rectangles, 4½" x 8½", for alternate blocks
- 2 strips, 2½" x 42"; crosscut strips into 20 squares, 2½" x 2½", for Star blocks
- 5 strips, 2¾" x 42", for outer border

From the pale yellow fabric, cut:

- 3 strips, 2½" x 42"; crosscut strips into 40 squares, 2½" x 2½", for Star blocks

From the gold fabric, cut:

- 4 strips, 4½" x 42"; crosscut strips into 32 squares, 4½" x 4½", for alternate blocks

From the yellow plaid, cut:

- 4 strips, 2½" x 42", for inner border

From the navy blue solid, cut:

- 3 squares, 13" x 13", for half-square triangle units in middle border

From the assorted yellow or gold fabrics, cut:

- 3 squares, 13" x 13", for half-square triangle units in middle border

Making the Star Blocks

1. Referring to "Making Folded-Corner Triangles" on page 12, sew a creased 2½" pale yellow square to opposite corners of a 2½" x 4½" navy blue rectangle as shown. Make 20 star points.

Make 20.

2. Assemble the star-point units and the 2½" and 4½" squares as shown to make a Star block. Make 5 blocks.

Make 5.

Making the Alternate Blocks and Half Blocks

1. Referring to "Making Folded-Corner Triangles" on page 12, sew a creased 4½" gold square to each corner of a 6³⁄₁₆" navy blue square as shown to make an alternate block. Make 4 blocks.

Make 4.

2. Sew a creased 4½" gold square to opposite corners of a 4½" x 8½" navy blue rectangle as shown to make an alternate half block. Make 8 half blocks.

Make 8.

Assembling the Quilt Top

1. Referring to the diagram below, arrange the blocks and alternate blocks as shown below.

2. Referring to "Making Straight-Set Quilts" on page 15, pin and sew the blocks together in horizontal rows. Pin and sew the rows together, matching the seams.

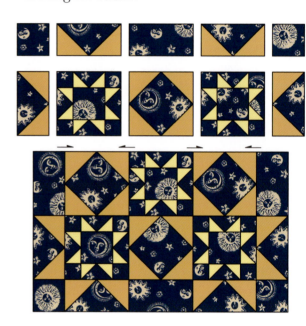

3. Referring to "Straight-Sewn Borders" on page 17, measure the quilt, trim, and sew the 2½"-wide inner border strips to the quilt top.

4. To make the sawtooth borders, refer to "Making Half-Square Triangle Units" on pages 12–14, and use the 13" squares of navy blue and yellow to make 76 navy-and-yellow half-square triangle units.

   Cut the bias strips 2½" wide.
   Cut the segments 2½" wide.
   Cut the squares 2½" x 2½".

Make 76.

5. Sew 18 half-square triangle units together as shown to make each of 4 border strips as shown. Add a half-square triangle unit to each end of 2 of the border strips, rotating the unit as shown.

Make 2.

Make 2.

6. Sew an 18-unit sawtooth border to each side of the quilt top, orienting the navy blue triangles toward the center of the quilt top. Press the seams toward the plaid strips. Sew a 20-unit sawtooth border to the top and bottom edges. Press the seams toward the plaid strips.

7. Referring to "Joining Border Strips" on page 17, sew the 2¾"-wide outer border strips end to end as needed. Referring to "Straight-Sewn Borders" on page 17, measure the quilt, trim, and sew the outer border strips to the quilt top.

Finishing the Quilt

1. Layer the quilt top, batting, and backing; baste. Quilt as desired.

2. Trim the batting and backing even with the edges of the quilt top. Sew the binding to the edges of the quilt.

3. Make and attach a label to your finished quilt.

Half-Square Triangle Units

Contrary Wife and Ornery Husband

CONTRARY WIFE AND ORNERY HUSBAND by Mary Hickey, Keyport, Washington, 1999.
Machine quilted by Sam Prescott.

The traditional Contrary Wife block, an easy Nine Patch with only four triangle pairs, blossoms into an elegant woven pattern when combined with the humble Snowball block. The key is careful color placement. Half of the Contrary Wife blocks are made in blue and half are made in red. Stitch this fresh simple design in traditional colors or consider sewing it with dazzling contemporary fabrics. If you have a slightly ornery nature, you can sneak a few gold and green triangles into the blocks. —MH

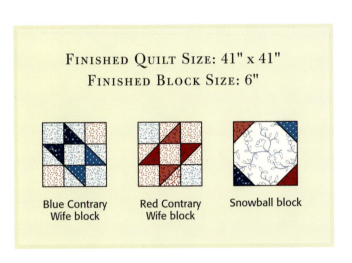

FINISHED QUILT SIZE: 41" x 41"
FINISHED BLOCK SIZE: 6"

Blue Contrary
Wife block

Red Contrary
Wife block

Snowball block

Materials 42"-wide fabric

* ½ yd. light blue print for Contrary Wife blocks
* ½ yd. light red print for Contrary Wife blocks
* ¼ yd. each of 3 assorted dark blue prints for Contrary Wife and Snowball blocks
* ¼ yd. each of 3 assorted dark red prints for Contrary Wife and Snowball blocks
* ⅔ yd. very light blue print for Snowball blocks
* ¼ yd. dark red print for inner border
* ⅔ yd. dark blue floral print for outer border
* 2½ yds. for backing
* 45" x 45" piece of batting
* ½ yd. dark blue for binding

Cutting

ALL MEASUREMENTS include ¼"-wide seam allowances.

From the light blue print, cut:
* 3 squares, 8" x 8", for half-square triangle units
* 2 strips, 2½" x 42"; crosscut strips into 30 squares, 2½" x 2½"

From the light red print, cut:
* 3 squares, 8" x 8", for half-square triangle units
* 2 strips, 2½" x 42"; crosscut strips into 30 squares, 2½" x 2½"

From the assorted dark blue prints, cut a total of:
* 3 squares, 8" x 8", for half-square triangle units
* 26 squares, 2½" x 2½"

From the assorted dark red prints, cut a total of:
* 3 squares, 8" x 8", for half-square triangle units
* 26 squares, 2½" x 2½"

From the very light blue print, cut:
* 13 squares, 6½" x 6½", for Snowball blocks

From the dark red print, cut:
* 4 strips, 1½" x 42", for inner border

From the dark blue floral print, cut:
* 4 strips, 4¾" x 42", for outer border

Making the Contrary Wife Blocks

1. Referring to "Making Half-Square Triangle Units" on pages 12–14, use the 8" light blue and dark blue squares to make 24 blue half-square triangle units. Repeat with the 8" light red and dark red squares to make 24 red half-square triangle units.

   Cut the bias strips 2½" wide.
   Cut the segments 2½" wide.
   Cut the squares 2½" x 2½".

   Make 24. Make 24.

2. Assemble the half-square triangle units and 2½" light squares as shown to make each of 6 blue blocks and 6 red blocks.

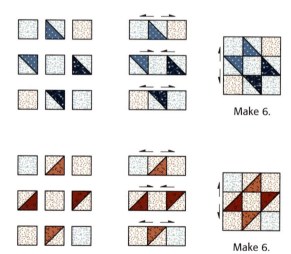

   Make 6.

   Make 6.

Making the Snowball Blocks

REFERRING TO "Making Folded-Corner Triangles" on page 12, sew 2 creased 2½" dark red squares to opposite diagonal corners of a very light blue 6½" square. Sew 2 creased 2½" dark blue squares to the remaining corners. Make 13 Snowball blocks.

   Make 13.

Assembling the Quilt Top

1. Referring to the diagram below, arrange the blocks in 5 horizontal rows of 5 blocks each.

2. Referring to "Making Straight-Set Quilts" on page 15, pin and sew the blocks together in horizontal rows. Carefully pin and sew the rows together, matching the seams.

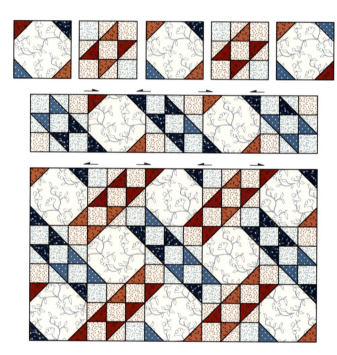

3. Referring to "Straight-Sewn Borders" on page 17, measure the quilt, trim, and sew the 1½"-wide inner border strips to the quilt top.

4. Repeat step 3 with the 4¾"-wide outer border strips.

Finishing the Quilt

1. Layer the quilt top, batting, and backing; baste. Quilt as desired.

2. Trim the batting and backing even with the edges of the quilt top. Sew the binding to the edges of the quilt.

3. Make and attach a label to your finished quilt.

Old-Fashioned Churn Dash

OLD-FASHIONED CHURN DASH by Joan Hanson, Seattle, Washington, 1997.

For decades, quilters have made scrap quilts both by necessity and because they are so interesting to design and make. Also, most quilters have such an obsession with shopping for and owning vast quantities of fabric that even if a small piece of a fabric is used, the purchase can be justified.

Successful scrap quilts often have a color recipe or plan so there is some organization to the controlled chaos of arranging all the scrappy fabrics. In this quilt, for example, the Churn Dash blocks all have a light viney print for the background, light to dark green triangles, and light pink to dark red rectangles. The alternating plain blocks vary from light to quite dark.

Part of the joy of making a scrap quilt for us is playing around with the placement of the colors. We enjoy arranging and rearranging blocks on our design wall and squinting at them through a reducing glass until the colors dance in a wonderful rhythm. We hope you have many happy hours rummaging through your fabric collection as well as your favorite quilt shops, finding fabrics to create your own scrappy version of this old favorite. —JH

FINISHED QUILT SIZE: 60½" x 71"
FINISHED BLOCK SIZE: 7½"

Churn Dash block

Materials 42"-wide fabric

NOTE: *Fat quarters, 18" x 22" pieces sold in quilt shops, are a great choice for this project.*

* 1½ yds. *total* assorted light floral prints for background in blocks
* ½ yd. *total* assorted pink and red prints for rectangles in blocks
* 1 yd. *total* assorted green prints for triangles in blocks
* 1½ yds. *total* assorted light and medium prints for plain blocks, side triangles, and corner triangles
* ½ yd. red print for inner border
* 2⅛ yds. light floral border stripe for middle border
* 1¼ yds. green print for outer border
* 3⅞ yds. for backing (pieced crosswise)
* 65" x 75" piece of batting
* ¾ yd. for binding

Cutting

ALL MEASUREMENTS include ¼"-wide seam allowances.

From the assorted light floral prints, cut a total of:
- 20 squares, 3" x 3", for block centers
- 6 strips, 1¾" x 42", for block side units
- 6 squares, 12" x 12", for half-square triangle units

From the assorted pink and red prints, cut a total of:
- 6 strips, 1¾" x 42", for block side units

From the assorted green prints, cut a total of:
- 6 squares, 12" x 12", for half-square triangle units

From the assorted light and medium prints, cut a total of:
- 12 squares, 8" x 8", for plain blocks
- 4 squares, 13" x 13"; cut squares twice diagonally to make 16 side setting triangles (you will only use 14)
- 2 squares, 7½" x 7½"; cut squares once diagonally to make 4 corner setting triangles

From the red print, cut:
- 8 strips, 1¾" x 42", for inner border

From the light floral border stripe, cut along the lengthwise grain:
- 2 strips, 4" x 74", for middle side borders
- 2 strips, 4" x 64", for middle top and bottom borders

From the green print, cut:
- 8 strips, 4½" x 42", for outer border

Making the Blocks

1. Sew a 1¾"-wide light floral strip to a 1¾"-wide pink or red strip as shown to make a strip set. Make 6 strip sets. Crosscut the strip sets into 80 segments, 3" wide, for the side units.

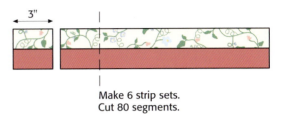

Make 6 strip sets.
Cut 80 segments.

2. Referring to "Making Half-Square Triangle Units" on pages 12–14, use the 12" light floral squares and green print squares to make 80 half-square triangle units.

    Cut the bias strips 3" wide.
    Cut the segments 3" wide.
    Cut the squares 3" x 3".

Make 80.

3. Using units with like fabrics, assemble 4 side units, 4 triangle units, and 1 light floral 3" square as shown to make a Churn Dash block. Make 20 blocks.

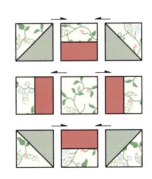
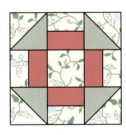

Make 20.

Assembling the Quilt Top

1. Referring to the diagram below, arrange the Churn Dash blocks, plain blocks, side setting triangles, and corner setting triangles in a pleasing and balanced color arrangement.

2. Referring to "Making Diagonal-Set Quilts" on pages 15–16, pin and sew the blocks together in diagonal rows. Press the seams toward the plain blocks and side setting triangles. Pin and sew the rows together, matching the seams. Use a long ruler to trim the edges ¼" from the block points.

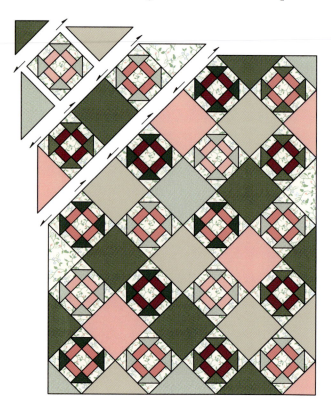

3. Referring to "Joining Border Strips" on page 17, sew the border strips end to end. Referring to "Borders with Mitered Corners" on pages 18–19, sew the inner, middle, and outer border strips together. Make 2 side border units and a top and a bottom border unit. Sew the border units to the quilt top. Miter the corners.

Make 2 side borders and a top and a bottom border.

Finishing the Quilt

1. Layer the quilt top, batting, and backing; baste. Quilt as desired.

2. Trim the batting and backing even with the edges of the quilt top. Sew the binding to the edges of the quilt.

3. Make and attach a label to your finished quilt.

Grandpa's Brown Bear Paws

GRANDPA'S BROWN BEAR PAWS by Mary Hickey, Seattle, Washington, 2000.

Machine quilted by Frankie Schmitt.

The idea of a Brown Bear Paw quilt just seems right. However, a gift from another quilter inspired the color scheme for this quilt. I used an exquisite William Morris reproduction "fat quarter," folded inside a fat greeting card, for the large squares in the Bear Paws.

The colors and design all make me think of my grandfather—a solid, sturdy, and utterly trustworthy man. He and my cousin Dan went canoe camping on the rivers of Missouri ten months out of every year. Whenever I smell sawdust, I see his fishing gear stacked near the back door, ready to take off at a moment's notice. The scent of wood smoke and barbecue sauce conjure up his ruddy smiling face, his eyes twinkling in anticipation of our oohs and ahs over the delicious dinner. An architect by profession, he worked at his drafting table on a screened porch, next to a wood stove in the winter and under a ceiling fan in the summer. He was a stable, kind, and creative influence in my children's upbringing. —MH

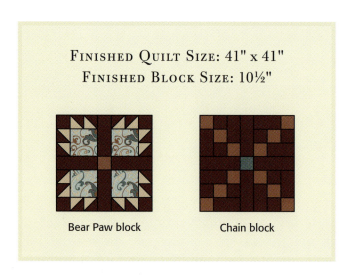

FINISHED QUILT SIZE: 41" x 41"
FINISHED BLOCK SIZE: 10½"

Bear Paw block   Chain block

Materials 42"-wide fabric

* 1¼ yds. brown print for Bear Paw blocks and Chain blocks
* ¼ yd. William Morris print for squares in Bear Paw blocks (or 1 fat quarter)
* ½ yd. light gold print for triangles in Bear Paw blocks
* ⅜ yd. dark gold print for Bear Paw blocks and Chain blocks
* ⅝ yd. green print for Chain block centers and outer border
* ⅜ yd. light tan print for inner border
* 2¾ yds. for backing
* 45" x 45" piece of batting
* ½ yd. for binding

Cutting

ALL MEASUREMENTS include ¼"-wide seam allowances.

From the brown print, cut:
* 2 squares, 15" x 15", for half-square triangles
* 2 strips, 3½" x 42", for Chain blocks
* 8 strips, 2" x 42"; cut 5 strips into 36 rectangles, 2" x 5", for Bear Paw blocks and Chain blocks; cut 1 strip into 20 squares, 2" x 2", for Bear Paw blocks; set aside 2 strips for Chain blocks

From the William Morris print, cut:
* 4 strips, 3½" x 21"; crosscut strips into 20 squares, 3½" x 3½", for Bear Paw blocks

From the light gold print, cut:
* 2 squares, 15" x 15", for half-square triangles

From the dark gold print, cut:
* 5 squares, 2" x 2", for Bear Paw blocks
* 3 strips, 2" x 42", for Chain blocks

From the green print, cut:
* 4 squares, 2" x 2", for Chain blocks
* 4 strips, 3½" x 42", for outer border

From the light tan print, cut:
* 4 strips, 2" x 42", for inner border

Making the Bear Paw Blocks

1. Referring to "Making Half-Square Triangle Units" on pages 12–14, use the 15" brown and light gold squares to make 80 half-square triangle units as follows:

   Cut the bias strips 2" wide.
   Cut the segments 2" wide.
   Cut the squares 2" x 2".

Make 80.

2. Assemble the half-square triangle units, 2" and 3½" squares, and 2" x 5" rectangles as shown to make a Bear Paw block. Make 5 blocks.

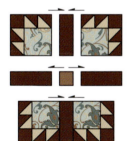

Make 5.

Making the Chain Blocks

1. Sew the 2"-wide dark gold strips, 2"-wide brown strips, and 3½"-wide brown strips together as shown to make strip sets A and B. Make 2 of strip set A and 1 of strip set B. Crosscut strip set A into 32 segments, 2" wide. Crosscut strip set B into 16 segments, 2" wide.

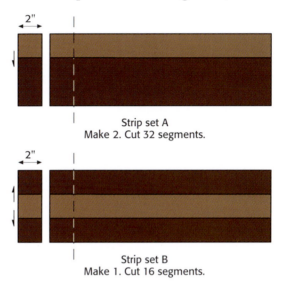

2. Assemble 2 A segments and 1 B segment as shown to make a nine-patch unit. Make 16 units.

Make 16.

3. Assemble the nine-patch units, 2" square, and 2" x 5" rectangles as shown to make a Chain block. Make 4 blocks.

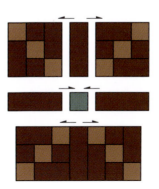

Make 4.

Assembling the Quilt Top

1. Referring to the diagram below, arrange the blocks in 3 horizontal rows of 3 blocks each.

2. Referring to "Making Straight-Set Quilts" on page 15, sew the blocks together in horizontal rows. Carefully pin and sew the rows together, matching the seams.

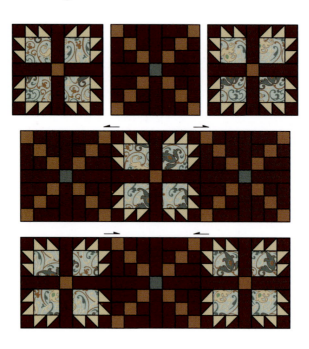

3. Referring to "Straight-Sewn Borders" on page 17, measure the quilt, trim, and sew the 2"-wide inner border strips to the quilt top.

4. Repeat step 3 with the 3½"-wide outer border strips.

Finishing the Quilt

1. Layer the quilt top, batting, and backing; baste. Quilt as desired.

2. Trim the batting and backing even with the edges of the quilt top. Sew the binding to the edges of the quilt.

3. Make and attach a label to your finished quilt.

Beach Blues

BEACH BLUES by Joan Hanson, Seattle, Washington, 2000.

This humble little block has many names and just as many ways that it can be used in a quilt design. It has been called Railroad Crossing, Jacob's Ladder, Going to Chicago, and most commonly, Buckeye Beauty. Like a Log Cabin block, it is a mirror image of itself when folded in half on the diagonal. This means that each block can be rotated when placed in a design to create lots of different design possibilities. Or as in Beach Blues, half the blocks have the dark blue triangles on the outside of the block and the other half have the light blue triangles on the outside. This creates the dramatic diagonal blue stripe effect. Before you stitch your blocks together, try several different arrangements on your design wall and perhaps you will come up with another version all your own.

Sometimes, when I start cutting strips, it's hard to know when to stop and I end up with twice as many of something as I really need. What a great opportunity to start a new project! This quilt began as a way to use up some leftover little red-and-white four patches. While trying to come up with a way to use them, I ran across a packet of fat quarters of lovely indigo blue fabrics that complemented the reds. Then while rummaging through my own fabrics to fill in a few pieces, I ran across the floral fabric in the border. I had been saving it for many years for just the right project. It seemed destined for this quilt, especially when a 5" square was all that was left over after I finished the border.

Mary and I spent two warm, sunny days last summer at my family's beach cabin. In addition to pulling crab pots, watching the baseball All-Star game, and lots of giggling and laughing, I finished making this quilt. I named this quilt "Beach Blues" to hold tight a delightful memory. —JH

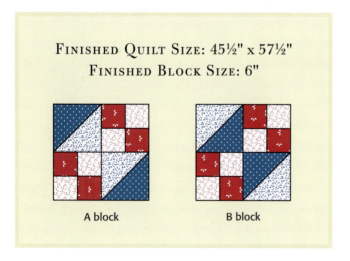

FINISHED QUILT SIZE: 45½" x 57½"
FINISHED BLOCK SIZE: 6"

A block   B block

Materials 42"-wide fabric

* 6 fat quarters of assorted dark blue prints
* 6 fat quarters of assorted light blue prints
* ½ yd. *total* of assorted dark pink and red prints
* ½ yd. *total* of assorted white and light pink prints
* ¼ yd. red print for inner border
* ¾ yd. floral print for middle border
* 1¼ yds. blue print for outer border and binding
* 2⅞ yds. for backing
* 50" x 62" piece of batting

Cutting

ALL MEASUREMENTS include ¼"-wide seam allowances.

From each of the dark blue and light blue fat quarters, cut:
- 1 square, 12½" x 12½" (12 total), for half-square triangle units

From the assorted dark pink and red prints, cut a total of:
- 7 strips, 2" x 42", for four-patch units

From the assorted white and light pink prints, cut a total of:
- 7 strips, 2" x 42", for four-patch units

From the red print, cut:
- 4 strips, 1¼" x 42, for inner border

From the floral print, cut:
- 5 strips, 4½" x 42", for middle border

From the blue print, cut:
- 5 strips, 3¼" x 42", for outer border

Making the Blocks

1. Referring to "Making Half-Square Triangle Units" on pages 12–14, use the 12½" dark blue and light blue squares to make 70 half-square triangle units as follows:

   Cut the bias strips 3½" wide.
   Cut the segments 3½" wide.
   Cut the squares 3½" x 3½".

Make 70.

2. Sew a 2"-wide dark pink or red strip to a 2"-wide white or light pink strip as shown to make a strip set. Make 7 strip sets. Crosscut the strip sets into 140 segments, 2" wide.

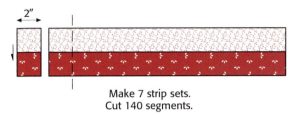

Make 7 strip sets.
Cut 140 segments.

3. Assemble 2 segments as shown to make a four-patch unit. Make 70 units.

Make 70.

4. Assemble 2 triangle units and 2 four-patch units as shown to make A and B blocks. Make 18 A blocks. Make 17 B blocks.

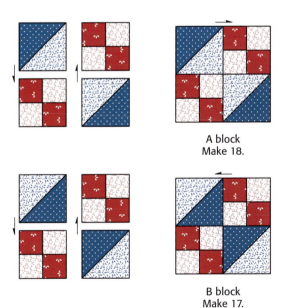

A block
Make 18.

B block
Make 17.

Assembling the Quilt Top

1. Referring to the diagram below, arrange the blocks in 7 horizontal rows of 5 blocks each.

2. Referring to "Making Straight-Set Quilts" on page 15, sew the blocks together in horizontal rows. Carefully pin and sew the rows together, matching the seams.

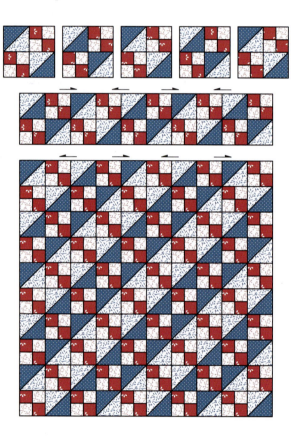

3. Referring to "Joining Border Strips" on page 17, sew the 1¼"-wide inner border strips together end to end as needed. Referring to "Straight-Sewn Borders" on page 17, measure the quilt, trim, and sew the inner border strips to the quilt top.

4. Repeat step 3 with the 4½"-wide middle border strips and the 3¼"-wide outer border strips.

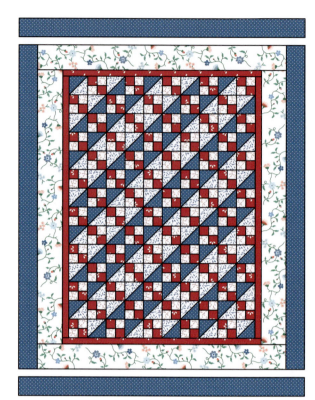

Finishing the Quilt

1. Layer the quilt top, batting, and backing; baste. Quilt as desired.

2. Trim the batting and backing even with the edges of the quilt top. Sew the binding to the edges of the quilt.

3. Make and attach a label to your finished quilt.

North Wind

NORTH WIND by Mary Hickey, Seattle, Washington, 2000.

Hand quilted by Anna Hostetler.

O nce in a while, a fabric just jumps off the shelf and lands in my arms ready to become a border. This happens often with periwinkle blue. When this occurs, I better make a quilt to go with the border and I better start right away because the fabric will call to me like snickerdoodles from the cookie jar.

I begin by picking out fabrics that match the colors in the border fabric. This usually covers the four primaries (red, yellow, blue, and green). I find it hard to work with only four colors so I often add one more color, such as turquoise, magenta, orange, or purple. In this quilt I added turquoise. Notice that the colors with more powerful light rays—red and yellow—appear fewer times in the quilt, while blue, green, and turquoise with quieter light rays appear in much greater numbers. The imbalance in these numbers provides the visual balance in the quilt. —MH

FINISHED QUILT SIZE: 70½" x 70½"
FINISHED BLOCK SIZE: 9"

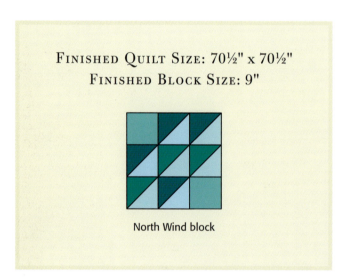

North Wind block

Materials 42"-wide fabric

* 1 fat quarter each of 2 dark yellows for blocks
* 1 fat quarter each of 2 light yellows for blocks
* ⅛ yd. medium yellow for block corners
* 1 fat quarter each of 2 dark reds for blocks
* 1 fat quarter each of 2 light reds for blocks
* ¼ yd. medium red for block corners
* 1 fat quarter each of 2 dark turquoises for blocks
* 1 fat quarter each of 2 light turquoises for blocks
* ¼ yd. medium turquoise for block corners
* 1 fat quarter each of 3 dark greens for blocks
* 1 fat quarter each of 3 light greens for blocks
* ¼ yd. medium green for block corners
* 1 fat quarter each of 4 dark blues for blocks
* 1 fat quarter each of 4 light blues for blocks
* ¼ yd. medium blue for block corners
* 1 yd. dark blue for inner and outer borders
* 1½ yds. blue floral print for middle border
* 4¼ yds. for backing
* 75" x 75" piece of batting
* ¾ yd. for binding

Cutting

ALL MEASUREMENTS include ¼"-wide seam allowances.

From each of the dark yellow and light yellow fat quarters, cut:

- 1 square, 12½" x 12½" (4 squares total), for half-square triangles

From the medium yellow, cut:

- 1 strip, 3½" x 21; crosscut strip into 6 squares, 3½" x 3½", for block corners

From each of the dark red and light red fat quarters, cut:

- 1 square, 18" x 18" (4 squares total), for half-square triangles

From the medium red, cut:

- 1 strip, 3½" x 42"; crosscut strip into 12 squares, 3½" x 3½", for block corners

From each of the dark turquoise and light turquoise fat quarters, cut:

- 1 square, 18" x 18" (4 squares total), for half-square triangles

From the medium turquoise, cut:

- 1 strip, 3½" x 42"; crosscut strip into 12 squares, 3½" x 3½", for block corners

From each of the dark green and light green fat quarters, cut:

- 1 square, 18" x 18" (6 squares total), for half-square triangles

From the medium green, cut:

- 2 strips, 3½" x 42"; crosscut strips into 18 squares, 3½" x 3½", for block corners

From each of the dark blue and light blue fat quarters, cut:

- 1 square, 18" x 18" (8 squares total), for half-square triangles

From the medium blue, cut:

- 2 strips, 3½" x 42"; crosscut strips into 24 squares, 3½" x 3½", for block corners

From the dark blue, cut:

- 13 strips, 2" x 42", for inner and outer borders

From the blue floral print, cut:

- 7 strips, 5½" x 42", for middle border

Making the Blocks

1. Referring to "Making Half-Square Triangle Units" on pages 12–14, use the 12½" dark yellow and light yellow squares to make 21 half-square triangle units as follows:

   Cut the bias strips 3½" wide.
   Cut the segments 3½" wide.
   Cut the squares 3½" x 3½".

Make 21 yellow.

2. Repeat step 1 with the 18" squares of the other colors, pairing a light and dark square of each color to make the triangle units. Make 42 red units, 42 turquoise units, 63 green units, and 84 blue units.

Make 42 red. Make 42 turquoise. Make 63 green. Make 84 blue.

3. Using the units and squares in the same color family, assemble 7 triangle units and 2 squares as shown to make a North Wind block. Make 3 yellow blocks, 6 red blocks, 6 turquoise blocks, 9 green blocks, and 12 blue blocks.

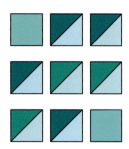

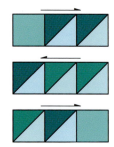

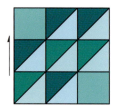

Make 3 yellow blocks, 6 red blocks, 6 turquoise blocks, 9 green blocks, and 12 blue blocks.

Assembling the Quilt Top

1. Referring to the diagram above right, arrange the blocks in 6 horizontal rows of 6 blocks each.

2. Referring to "Making Straight-Set Quilts" on page 15, pin and sew the blocks together in horizontal rows. Carefully pin and sew the rows together, matching the seams.

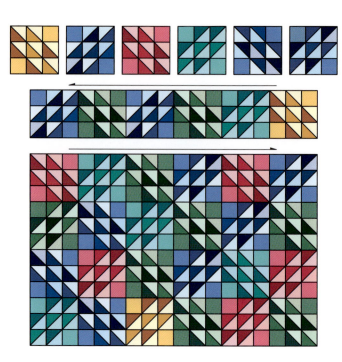

3. Referring to "Joining Border Strips" on page 17, sew the border strips together end to end. Referring to "Borders with Mitered Corners" on pages 18–19, sew the inner, middle, and outer border strips together, making 4 border units. Sew the border units to the quilt top. Miter the corners.

Finishing the Quilt

1. Layer the quilt top, batting, and backing; baste. Quilt as desired.

2. Trim the batting and backing even with the edges of the quilt top. Sew the binding to the edges of the quilt.

3. Make and attach a label to your finished quilt.

Andrew and Patrick Sail Away

ANDREW AND PATRICK SAIL AWAY by Joan Hanson, Seattle, Washington, 2000.

From the collection of Andrew and Patrick Hanson.

My nephew and his wife recently had twin boys, Andrew and Patrick. Since they were decorating with a nautical theme, I decided to make them each a Sailboat quilt. I started with the blue stripe for the water sashing and the blue-and-white dot fabric for the border, a decorator fabric I had used to make a valance for my son Derek's room. Next I found the red-and-white anchor fabric and the blue sky fabric. (The sky fabric needs to be dark enough to contrast with the white sails and light enough to contrast with the bright sailboats.)

The colorful boat fabric came from my stash. Since I also wanted to have a quilt of my own, I ended up making three quilts. For Andrew and Patrick's quilts, I embroidered their names on a sail in each quilt. Everything was going according to plan until I got halfway through the second quilt and ran out of the blue-and-white dot fabric. I'm sure you can guess what I did next. Since Derek had just left for college, I didn't think he would notice if his window was bare . . . and so far, he hasn't. —JH

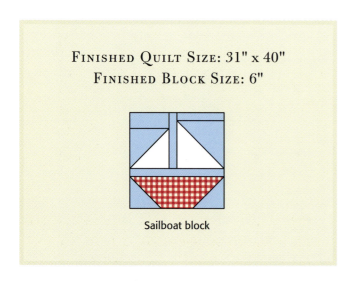

FINISHED QUILT SIZE: 31" x 40"
FINISHED BLOCK SIZE: 6"

Sailboat block

Materials 42"-wide fabric

* ⅞ yd. blue sky fabric for Sailboat blocks
* ½ yd. white sail fabric for Sailboat blocks
* ¼ yd. *total* of assorted bright scraps for sailboats
* ⅓ yd. water fabric for horizontal sashing strips
* ¼ yd. red print for inner border
* ¾ yd. navy blue print for outer border and binding
* 1¼ yds. for backing
* 35" x 44" piece of batting

Cutting

ALL MEASUREMENTS include ¼"-wide seam allowances.

From the blue sky fabric, cut:
* 2 squares, 12" x 12", for half-square triangle units
* 24 squares, 2½" x 2½", for piece D
* 12 rectangles, 1" x 3½", for piece E
* 12 rectangles, 1" x 4", for piece F
* 12 rectangles, 1½" x 3", for piece G
* 12 rectangles, 1" x 6½", for piece H
* 8 strips, 2" x 6½", for vertical sashing strips

From the white sail fabric, cut:
* 1 square, 12" x 12", for half-square triangle units (A)
* 1 square, 12½" x 12½", for half-square triangle units (B)

From the assorted bright scraps, cut:
* 12 rectangles, 2½" x 6½", for piece C

From the water fabric, cut:
* 4 strips, 2" x 21½", for horizontal sashing strips

From the red print, cut:
* 4 strips, 1½" x 42", for inner border

From the navy blue print, cut:
* 4 strips, 4¼" x 42", for outer border

Making the Blocks

1. Referring to "Making Half-Square Triangle Units" on pages 12–14, pair a 12" blue sky and white sail square to make 12 half-square triangle units (A) as follows:

   Cut the bias strips 3" wide.
   Cut the segments 3" wide.
   Cut the squares 3" x 3".

   Make 12.

2. Use the 12½" blue sky and white sail squares to make 12 half-square triangle units (B) as follows:

   Cut the bias strips 3½"wide.
   Cut the segments 3½" wide.
   Cut the squares 3½" x 3½".

   Make 12.

3. Referring to "Making Folded-Corner Triangles" on page 12, sew a creased 2½" blue sky square (D) to opposite ends of the 2½" x 6½" boat pieces (C) to make 12 boat units.

   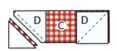
   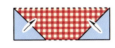

   Make 12.

4. Assemble the pieces for each block as shown. Make 12 blocks.

   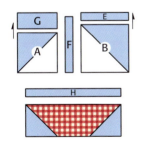
   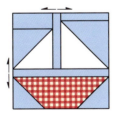

   Make 12.

Assembling the Quilt Top

1. Referring to the diagram below, arrange the blocks in 4 horizontal rows of 3 blocks and 2 vertical sashing strips each.

2. Referring to "Making Straight-Set Quilts" on page 15, pin and sew the blocks and sashing strips together in horizontal rows. Carefully pin and sew the rows together, adding a horizontal sashing strip between the rows.

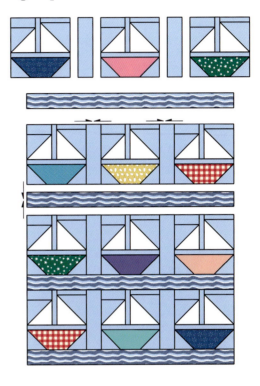

3. Referring to "Straight-Sewn Borders" on page 17, measure the quilt, trim, and sew the 1½"-wide inner border strips to the quilt top.

4. Repeat step 3 with the 4¼"-wide outer border strips.

Finishing the Quilt

1. Layer the quilt top, batting, and backing; baste. Quilt as desired.

2. Trim the batting and backing even with the edges of the quilt top. Sew the binding to the edges of the quilt.

3. Make and attach a label to your finished quilt.

Red Union Square

RED UNION SQUARE by Mary Hickey, Seattle, Washington, 2000.

Hand quilted by Frances Yoder.

When I was a child, I would open my treasured box of crayons every morning to start the serious business of a five-year-old: coloring. The same problem occurred every day. All the crayons sat in their orderly ranks waiting for their turns. All but one. The red one was usually just a short little stub, barely graspable, lying lopsided in the bottom of the box. I operated on the serious philosophical principle "If it's red, it's pretty." I think many of us felt that way.

I still love red, but now I have red fabric rather than red crayons. And I have a lot of red fabric—boxes and boxes of glorious reds, crimsons, scarlets, burgundies, and cherries. When I want to make a red quilt or use red in a quilt, I have the fabric that I need. I just love to sit on the floor surrounded by little mountains of red fabric, choosing the shades I want for a quilt.

The toile in this quilt presented an interesting problem. It is directional. Up is up and looks annoying if it is sideways or upside down. So, I suggest that you either plan your cuts carefully or buy a random print that does not require so much planning. —MH

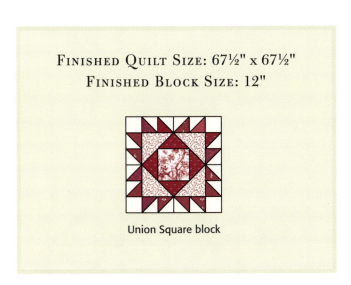

FINISHED QUILT SIZE: 67½" x 67½"
FINISHED BLOCK SIZE: 12"

Union Square block

Materials 42"-wide fabric

* 2 yds. red-and-white toile for pieced blocks, plain blocks, and outer border
* 3 yds. *total* of assorted dark red prints for pieced blocks and inner border
* ½ yd. medium red print for blocks
* 2 yds. white fabric for pieced blocks
* ¼ yd. dark red print for inner border
* 4⅛ yds. for backing
* 72" x 72" batting
* ⅝ yd. for binding

Cutting

ALL MEASUREMENTS include ¼"-wide seam allowances.

From the red-and-white toile, cut:
* 3 strips, 6" x 42", along crosswise grain for top and bottom outer borders
* 2 strips, 6" x 68", along lengthwise grain for side outer borders
* 9 squares, 4½" x 4½", for block centers
* 4 squares, 12½" x 12½", for plain squares

From the assorted dark red prints, cut a total of:
* 2 strips, 3¾" x 42"; crosscut strips into 18 squares, 3¾" x 3¾", then cut squares once diagonally to make 36 triangles
* 8 squares, 15" x 15", for half-square triangle units
* 2 squares, 19" x 19"; cut squares twice diagonally to make 8 side setting triangles
* 2 squares, 10" x 10"; cut squares once diagonally to make 4 corner setting triangles

From the medium red print, cut:
* 3 strips, 4⅞" x 42"; crosscut strips into 18 squares, 4⅞" x 4⅞", then cut squares once diagonally to make 36 triangles

From the white fabric, cut:

- 8 squares, 15" x 15", for half-square triangle units
- 3 strips, 2½" x 42"; crosscut strips into 36 squares, 2½" x 2½", for block corners

From the dark red print, cut:

- 5 strips, 1" x 42", for inner border

Making the Blocks

1. Sew a dark red 3¾" triangle to opposite sides of a 4½" toile square as shown. Sew a dark red triangle to the remaining sides of the square. Make 9 units.

Make 9.

2. Sew a medium red 4⅞" triangle to opposite sides of the unit made in step 1 as shown. Sew a medium red triangle to the remaining sides of the unit.

Make 9.

3. Referring to "Making Half-Square Triangle Units" on pages 12–14, pair the 15" white and dark red squares to make 252 half-square triangle units as follows:

> Cut the bias strips 2½" wide.
> Cut the segments 2½" wide.
> Cut the squares 2½" x 2½".

Make 252.

4. Select 144 triangle units for the blocks. Sew 4 units together as shown. Make 36 sections. Add a 2½" white square to each end of 18 of the 36 sections.

Make 18.   Make 18.

5. Assemble the center unit and triangle sections as shown to make a Union Square block. Make 9 blocks.

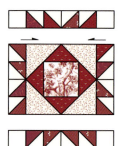 

Make 9.

Assembling the Quilt Top

1. Referring to the diagram on page 113, arrange the blocks, plain squares, and side and corner setting triangles in diagonal rows.

2. Referring to "Making Diagonal-Set Quilts" on pages 15–16, pin and sew the blocks together in diagonal rows. Carefully pin and sew the rows together, matching the seams. Use a long ruler to trim the edges of the quilt ¼" from the block points.

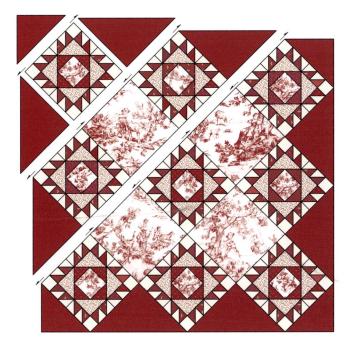

3. Referring to "Joining Border Strips" on page 17, sew the 1"-wide inner border strips together end to end as needed. Referring to "Straight-Sewn Borders" on page 17, measure the quilt, trim, and sew the inner border strips to the quilt top.

4. Using the remaining 108 triangle units, sew 26 units together as shown to make each of the side borders. Sew 28 triangle units together as shown to make each of the top and bottom borders, making sure to orient the triangle unit at each end correctly.

5. Sew a side border to opposite sides of the quilt. Press the seams toward the inner border. Sew the remaining borders to the top and bottom edges. Press the seams toward the inner border.

6. Referring to "Straight-Sewn Borders" on page 17, measure the quilt, trim, and sew the 6"-wide toile outer borders to the quilt. You will need to join the crosswise-cut strips before adding them to the top and bottom edges.

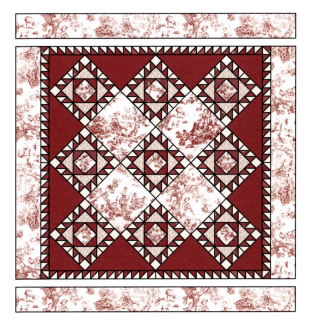

Finishing the Quilt

1. Layer the quilt top, batting, and backing; baste. Quilt as desired.

2. Trim the batting and backing even with the edges of the quilt top. Sew the binding to the edges of the quilt.

3. Make and attach a label to your finished quilt.

Make 2 side borders.

Make a top and a bottom border.

Hovering Hawks

HOVERING HAWKS by Mary Hickey, Seattle, Washington, 2000.

Hand quilted by Anna Hostetler.

Hovering Hawks is the proper name for the blocks in this quilt. But I prefer to call it Hovering Chicken after our chicken named Marsha. A lovely honey-colored tan with golden eyes, Marsha was really quite an athletic chicken. She liked to go for a little run every morning. She would stand very still for a few seconds, then streak across the lawn, come to an abrupt stop, and fall on her beak. Marsha also liked to walk up a little hill in our yard to a three-foot retaining wall. From the wall she would launch herself for a brief flight. She remained airborne only a fleeting second because her hip span was so large in comparison to her wingspan. Marsha emitted a sort of gleeful squawk (maybe it was terror) as she flapped on her downward flight. No matter how hard she flapped, she always hit pretty hard. She was plucky though, and got right up and marched with quiet pride back up to the wall for another try.

As Marsha aged, we found it harder to watch her brave flights, which by the time she was four years old consisted of a feathery crash accompanied by indignant clucks. She discovered that sitting on the porch swing was a bit like flying, and came a-running when anyone came along to give her a boost up to the swing seat.

By the time she was seven (which is quite ancient for a chicken), she really couldn't manage the flights anymore and often looked depressed when she walked along the retaining wall. That year, on a bitter cold December afternoon, we heard a terrific commotion in the yard and looked out in time to see Marsha racing toward the cliff edge of our yard above the beach. Soon we saw and heard a huge eagle, majestically gliding over the bay with an elderly golden chicken clutched in its talons, flying, at long last, flying east toward the forest.

Such a momentous event in a family's history had to be commemorated with a splendid quilt. We decided on the Hovering Hawks block and a sawtooth border. Yes, this did involve a lot of piecing, but all really easy piecing—no set-in seams or slender points. Making half-square triangles is a pleasant process, a little like making cookies. Put a good movie in the DVD player, oil up your machine, and make them as if you were cutting cookies. Stack them in groups of ten or twenty. Every time you reach one hundred, reward yourself with a real cookie. Soon you will have all the ingredients to make an award-winning quilt. —MH

FINISHED QUILT SIZE: 44½" x 44½"
FINISHED BLOCK SIZE: 8"

Hovering Hawks block

Materials 42"-wide fabric

✳ 1 fat quarter each of 6 assorted dark blue prints for blocks and middle pieced border
✳ 1 fat quarter each of 6 assorted light blue prints for blocks, inner border, and middle pieced border
✳ 1 fat quarter each of 3 assorted dark green prints for blocks and middle pieced border
✳ 1 fat quarter each of 3 assorted light green prints for blocks and middle pieced border
✳ 1 fat quarter each of 2 assorted dark red prints for blocks
✳ 1 fat quarter each of 2 assorted light red prints for blocks
✳ 1 fat quarter each of 1 dark brown print and 1 light brown print
✳ ½ yd. dark blue print for outer border
✳ 2⅞ yds. for backing
✳ 49" x 49" piece of batting
✳ ½ yd. for binding

Cutting

ALL MEASUREMENTS include ¼" seam allowances. Different-size squares are used for the half-square triangle units because each size results in a different yield.

From each of the dark blue prints, cut:
• 1 square, 12½" x 12½" (6 squares total)

From each of the light blue prints, cut:
• 1 square, 12½" x 12½" (6 squares total)

From the remainder of the light blue prints, cut a total of:
• 8 strips, 2½" x 21", for inner border
• 32 squares, 2½" x 2½"

From each of the dark green prints, cut:
• 1 square, 12½" x 12½" (3 squares total)

From each of the light green prints, cut:
• 1 square, 12½" x 12½" (3 squares total)

From the remainder of the light green prints, cut a total of:
• 26 squares, 2½" x 2½"

From each of the dark red prints, cut:
• 1 square, 10" x 10" (2 total)

From each of the light red prints, cut:
• 1 square, 10" x 10" (2 total)

From the remainder of the light red prints, cut a total of:
• 38 squares, 2½" x 2½"

From the dark brown print, cut:
• 1 square, 8" x 8"

From the light brown print, cut:
• 1 square, 8" x 8"

From the dark blue print, cut:
• 5 strips, 2½" x 42", for outer border

Making the Blocks

1. Referring to "Making Half-Square Triangle Units" on pages 12–14, pair the light and dark squares (8", 10", and 12½") to make half-square triangle units as follows:

> Cut the bias strips 2½" wide.
> Cut the segments 2½" wide.
> Cut the squares 2½" x 2½".

Make 132 blue triangle units, 70 green triangle units, 26 red triangle units, and 8 brown triangle units.

Make 132 blue. Make 70 green. Make 26 red. Make 8 brown.

2. Assemble 10 triangle units, 4 squares in the same color family and 2 squares in the opposite color family as shown to make a Hovering Hawks block. Make 13 blue-and-green blocks and 3 red-and-brown blocks.

Make 13 blue-and-green blocks.

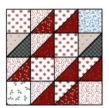

Make 3 red-and-brown blocks.

Assembling the Quilt Top

1. Referring to the diagram below, arrange the blocks in 4 horizontal rows of 4 blocks each.

2. Referring to "Making Straight-Set Quilts" on page 15, pin and sew the blocks together in horizontal rows. Carefully pin and sew the rows together, matching the seams.

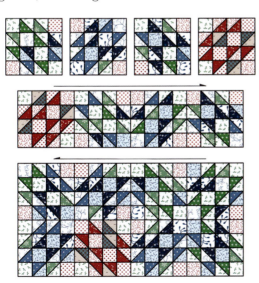

3. Using the remaining 76 blue-and-green triangle units, sew 18 units together as shown to make each of 4 borders. Sew a red triangle unit to each end of 2 of the borders for the top and bottom edges.

Make 2 side borders.

Make a top and a bottom border.

4. Referring to "Joining Border Strips" on page 17, sew the 2½" x 21" inner border strips in pairs end to end as needed. Referring to "Straight-Sewn Borders" on page 17, measure the quilt, trim, and sew the inner border strips to the quilt top.

5. Sew a pieced side border to opposite sides of the quilt top. Press the seams toward the inner border. Sew the remaining pieced borders to the top and bottom edges. Press the seams toward the inner border.

6. Referring to "Joining Border Strips" on page 17, sew the 2½"-wide outer border strips end to end as needed. Measure the quilt, trim, and sew the outer border strips to the quilt top. Press the seams toward the outer border strips.

Finishing the Quilt

1. Layer the quilt top, batting, and backing; baste. Quilt as desired.

2. Trim the batting and backing even with the edges of the quilt top. Sew the binding to the edges of the quilt.

3. Make and attach a label to your finished quilt.

Quarter-Square
Triangle Units

Floral Symphony

FLORAL SYMPHONY by Mary Hickey, Seattle, Washington, 2000.

Machine quilted by Frankie Schmitt.

Toward the end of winter, here in the great Pacific Northwest, the trees drip, the sun coughs behind the clouds, and the moss grows like a rash on our roofs. Everyone's skin turns to pasty gray and we, like all northerners, start to long for flowers and sunshine. We daydream of shorts, sunglasses, and sailboats. Even freckles sound appealing. Then, we look outside one day and notice that two or three brave camellias have optimistically blossomed under the sunless sky. Their bright pink color shines as a beacon on our moss-colored world. Within a few weeks, the ornamental plums, crab apples, and cherry trees announce to the tulips and daffodils that it's time, and signal the riotous resurgence of our lush landscape.

The lavish floral fabrics in this quilt do almost all of the work. By setting the blocks on-point with energetic florals and bordering them with even more flowers, the quilt takes on an aura of springtime grandeur. January is the time to pull out the boxes of floral fabric from under the bed and whip up this little garden of a quilt to remind our fog-clouded eyes of the coming spring. —MH

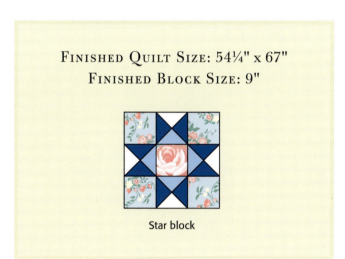

FINISHED QUILT SIZE: 54¼" x 67"
FINISHED BLOCK SIZE: 9"

Star block

Materials 42"-wide fabric

* 1 yd. white small-scale floral print for background of star points
* ½ yd. light blue print for background of star points
* 1 yd. dark blue print for star points
* 1⅜ yds. *total* assorted floral prints for block corners
* ¼ yd. *total* assorted floral prints for block centers
* ¾ yd. white large-scale floral print for plain squares
* 2¼ yds. medium blue floral print for side and corner setting triangles and outer border
* ¾ yd. pink floral print for inner border
* 3⅛ yds. for backing
* 58" x 71" piece of batting
* ⅝ yd. for binding

Cutting

ALL MEASUREMENTS include ¼"-wide seam allowances

From the white small-scale floral print, cut:
- 3 squares, 15" x 15", for quarter-square triangles

From the light blue print, cut:
- 2 squares, 15" x 15", for quarter-square triangles

From the dark blue print, cut:
- 5 squares, 15" x 15", for quarter-square triangles

From the assorted floral prints for block corners, cut a total of:
- 48 squares, 3½" x 3½" (you will need 4 matching squares for each block)

From the assorted floral prints for block centers, cut a total of:
- 12 squares, 3½" x 3½"

From the white large-scale floral print, cut:
- 6 squares, 9½" x 9½", for plain squares

From the medium blue floral print, cut:
- 3 squares, 15" x 15"; cut squares twice diagonally to create 12 side triangles (you will use only 10)
- 2 squares, 9" x 9"; cut squares once diagonally to create 4 corner triangles
- 7 strips, 6" x 42", for outer border

From the pink floral print, cut:
- 5 strips, 2½" x 42", for inner border

Making the Blocks

NOTE: *Look carefully at the color photo on page 120. Notice that the quarter-square triangle units in the star points have one white, one light blue, and two dark blue triangles in each unit. By making some of the strip units white and dark blue and some of them light blue and dark blue, you can easily make these triangle groups.*

1. Referring to "Making Quarter-Square Triangle Units" on page 14, use the 15" squares of white and dark blue to make 28 half-square triangle units as follows:

   Cut the bias strips 3⅞" wide.
   Cut the segments 3⅞" wide.
   Cut the squares 3⅞" x 3⅞".

   Cut the squares in half on the diagonal, perpendicular to the seam line, to make 56 halves.

Make 28.

2. Repeat step 1 with the 15" squares of light blue and dark blue to make 20 half-square triangle units. Cut the squares in half to make 40 halves.

Make 20.

3. Sew the half units from steps 1 and 2 together as shown to make the white star points and blue star points. Make 4 matching star points for each white and blue block.

Make 4 matching star points for each white-star block (total 8).

Make 4 matching star points for each blue-star block (total 40).

4. Assemble 4 star points, 4 floral corner squares, and 1 floral center square as shown to make a Star block. Make 2 blocks with white star points and 10 blocks with blue star points.

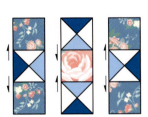

Make 2
white-star blocks.

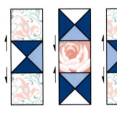

Make 10
blue-star blocks.

Assembling the Quilt Top

1. Referring to the diagram below, arrange the blocks and corner and side triangles in diagonal rows.

2. Referring to "Making Diagonal-Set Quilts" on pages 15–16, pin and sew the blocks together in diagonal rows. Carefully pin and sew the rows together, matching the seams. Use a long ruler to trim the edges of the quilt ¾" from the block points.

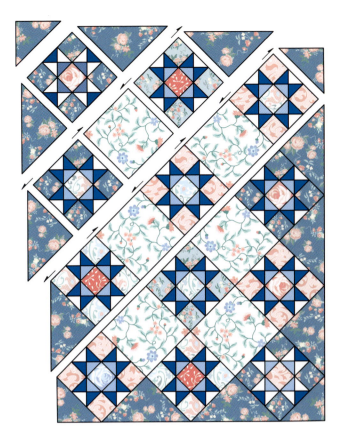

3. Referring to "Joining Border Strips" on page 17, sew the border strips end to end. Referring to "Borders with Mitered Corners" on pages 18–19, sew the inner and outer borders strips together. Make 4 border units. Sew the border units to the quilt top. Miter the corners.

Finishing the Quilt

1. Layer the quilt top, batting, and backing; baste. Quilt as desired.

2. Trim the batting and backing even with the edges of the quilt top. Sew the binding to the edges of the quilt.

3. Make and attach a label to your finished quilt.

Swedish Stepping Stars

SWEDISH STEPPING STARS by Mary Hickey, Seattle, Washington, 2000.

Machine quilted by Frankie Schmitt.

On gloomy, cold, misty winter afternoons, I love to light a fire in the fireplace and work on a quilt in summer colors—warm, buttery yellows, pale sky blues, and darker hydrangea blues. It takes some courage to mix humble little calicoes with a grand Jacobean decorator chintz, but the result is the lively, lighthearted quilt shown here.

Select a rich floral print in pale blues and yellows for the outer border. Take out your blue fabrics and your yellow fabrics and sort them into three stacks: pale yellows, light blues, and medium blues. Figure out which color should be in each spot on the star blocks. Make each star one at a time from your stack. Don't worry about the final quilt. Just work to make each block pretty and cheerful. Then do the same with the Stepping Stones blocks. Soon your quilt top will be ready for assembly. —MH

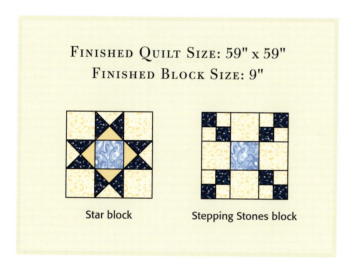

FINISHED QUILT SIZE: 59" x 59"
FINISHED BLOCK SIZE: 9"

Star block   Stepping Stones block

Materials 42"-wide fabric

* ¾ yd. each of 3 pale yellow prints for block backgrounds
* ½ yd. each of 3 dark blue prints for star points and stepping stones
* ¾ yd. *total* of assorted medium blue prints for block centers and corners
* ⅜ yd. dark blue print for inner border
* 1 yd. yellow-and-blue large-scale floral print for outer border
* 3⅝ yds. for backing
* 63" x 63" piece of batting
* ¾ yd. for binding

Cutting

ALL MEASUREMENTS include ¼"-wide seam allowances.

From 2 of the pale yellow prints, cut:
* 2 squares from each fabric, 15" x 15" (4 total), for quarter-square triangle units

From the third pale yellow print, cut:
* 1 square, 15" x 15" for quarter-square triangle units

From the remaining pieces of pale yellow prints, cut:
* 5 strips, 2" x 42", for four-patch units in Stepping Stones blocks
* 84 squares, 3½" x 3½", for Star blocks and Stepping Stones blocks (you will need 4 matching squares for each block)

From 2 of the dark blue prints, cut:
* 2 squares from each fabric, 15" x 15" (4 total), for quarter-square triangle units

From the third dark blue print, cut:
* 1 square, 15" x 15", for quarter-square triangle units

From the remaining pieces of dark blue prints, cut a total of:

- 5 strips, 2" x 42", for four-patch units in Stepping Stones blocks

From the assorted medium blue prints, cut a total of:

- 25 squares, 3½" x 3½", for block centers
- 16 squares, 3½" x 3½", for corners on Star blocks in outer corners of quilt top (you will need 4 matching squares for each block)

From the dark blue print, cut:

- 5 strips, 2" x 42", for inner border

From the yellow-and-blue floral print, cut:

- 5 strips, 5¾" x 42", for outer border

Making the Star Blocks

1. Referring to "Making Quarter-Square Triangle Units" on page 14, use the 15" pale yellow and dark blue squares to make 52 half-square triangle units as follows:

   Cut the strips 3⅞" wide.
   Cut the segments 3⅞" wide.
   Cut the squares 3⅞" x 3⅞".

   Cut the squares in half on the diagonal, perpendicular to the seam line, to make 104 halves.

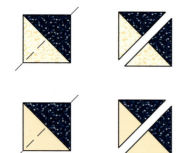

2. Sew 2 halves together so that the blue triangles match and the yellow triangles differ. Make 4 matching star points for each block.

Make 4 matching
star points
for each block
(52 total).

3. Assemble 4 triangle units, 4 yellow 3½" squares, and 1 medium blue 3½" square as shown to make a Star block. Make 9 blocks with yellow corners.

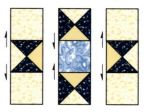

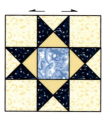

Make 9.

4. Assemble 4 triangle units and 5 medium blue 3½" squares as shown to make a Star block. Make 4 blocks with medium blue corners.

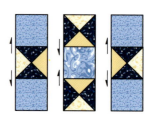

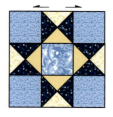

Make 4.

Making the Stepping Stones Blocks

1. Sew a 2" x 42" strip of yellow and dark blue together to make a strip set. Make 5 strip sets. Crosscut the strip sets into 96 segments, 2" wide.

Make 5 strip sets.
Cut 96 segments.

2. Sew 2 segments together as shown to make a four-patch unit. Make 48 units, 4 matching units for each block.

Make 48.

3. Using matching units, assemble the four-patch units and 3½" squares as shown to make a Stepping Stones block. Make 12 blocks.

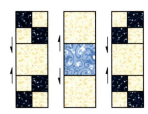

Make 12.

Assembling the Quilt Top

1. Referring to the diagram below, arrange the blocks in 5 horizontal rows of 5 blocks each.

2. Referring to "Making Straight-Set Quilts" on page 15, pin and sew the blocks together in horizontal rows. Carefully pin and sew the rows together, matching the seams.

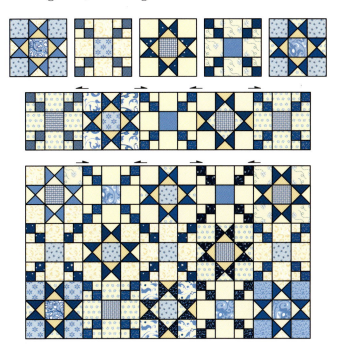

3. Referring to "Joining Border Strips" on page 17, sew the 2"-wide inner border strips together end to end. Referring to "Straight-Sewn Borders" on page 17, measure the quilt, trim, and sew the inner border strips to the quilt top.

4. Repeat step 3 with the 5¾"-wide outer border strips.

Finishing the Quilt

1. Layer the quilt top, batting, and backing; baste. Quilt as desired.

2. Trim the batting and backing even with the edges of the quilt top. Sew the binding to the edges of the quilt.

3. Make and attach a label to your finished quilt.

Beary, Beary Strawberry

BEARY, BEARY STRAWBERRY by Joan Hanson, Seattle, Washington, 1997.

The Bear Paw block is another classic that we have updated and simplified with easy rotary-cutting techniques. The easy half-square triangle method is used to make the "toes." Then the center "pad" for each "paw" is made with our easy quarter-square triangle method. This is a great project for trying out both of these techniques, since the pieces are large and easy to work with.

Most of the fabrics used in this quilt were from a collection that included the background fabric, striped border fabric, and the dark floral print used in the paw points. Using fabric collections gives a more coordinated look to your project than using many fabrics, which gives a scrappier look. I like to hang this quilt up at Christmas and often leave it up until after Valentine's Day. —JH

FINISHED QUILT SIZE: 48" x 48"
FINISHED BLOCK SIZE: 13½"

Bear Paw block

Materials 42"-wide fabric

* 1¼ yds. light print for block background and sashing
* 1 fat quarter each of 2 red prints for blocks
* 1 fat quarter each of 2 green prints for blocks
* ½ yd. dark print for "paw" points
* 1½ yds. border stripe for inner border
* ¾ yd. red print for outer border and binding
* 3 yds. fabric for backing
* 52" x 52" piece of batting

Cutting

ALL MEASUREMENTS include ¼"-wide seam allowances.

From the light print, cut:
* 2 squares, 15" x 15", for half-square triangle units
* 3 strips, 2" x 42"; crosscut strips into 16 rectangles, 2" x 6½", for blocks
* 6 strips, 2½" x 42"; crosscut strips into 12 rectangles, 2½" x 14", for sashing strips, and 16 squares, 2½" x 2½", for blocks

From the 2 red prints, cut:
* 1 square from each print, 12½" x 12½" (2 total), for quarter-square triangle units
* 4 squares, 2" x 2", for block centers
* 9 squares, 2½" x 2½", for sashing squares

From the 2 green prints, cut:
* 1 square from each print, 12½" x 12½" (2 total), for quarter-square triangle units

From the dark print, cut:
* 2 squares, 15" x 15", for half-square triangle units
* 4 squares, 2¾" x 2¾", for corner squares in outer border

From the border stripe, cut along the lengthwise grain:

- 4 strips, 5½" x 48", for inner border

From the red print, cut:

- 5 strips, 2¾" x 42", for outer border

Making the Blocks

1. Referring to "Making Quarter-Square Triangle Units" on page 14, pair the 12½" red squares to make 8 half-square triangle units as follows:

    Cut the bias strips 4⅞" wide.
    Cut the segments 4⅞" wide.
    Cut the squares 4⅞" x 4⅞".

    Cut the squares in half, perpendicular to the seam line, to make 16 halves.

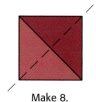

Make 8.

2. Repeat step 1 with the 12½" green squares.

Make 8.

3. Sew a red half unit and a green half unit together as shown to make a quarter-square triangle unit. Make 4 matching quarter-square triangle units for each block.

Make 4 matching quarter-square triangle units for each block (16 total).

4. Pair the 15" squares of light print and dark print to make 64 half-square triangle units for the "paw" points as follows:

    Cut the bias strips 2½" wide.
    Cut the segments 2½" wide.
    Cut the squares 2½" x 2½".

Make 64.

5. Assemble the half-square triangle units, quarter-square triangle units, 2" and 2½" squares, and 2" x 6½" rectangles as shown to make a Bear Paw block. Make 4 blocks.

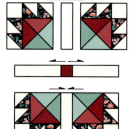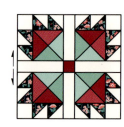

Make 4.

Assembling the Quilt Top

1. Referring to the diagram below, arrange the blocks in 2 horizontal rows of 2 blocks and 3 sashing strips each. Alternate with 3 rows of 3 sashing squares and 2 sashing strips.

2. Referring to "Making Straight-Set Quilts" on page 15, pin and sew units together in horizontal rows. Carefully pin and sew the rows together, matching the seams.

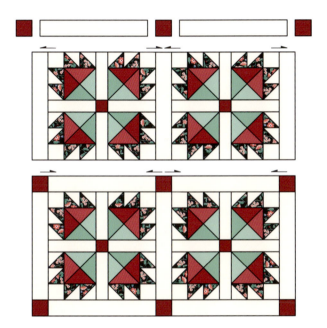

3. Referring to "Borders with Mitered Corners" on pages 18–19, measure the quilt, trim, and sew the 5½"-wide inner border strips to the quilt top, mitering the corners.

4. Referring to "Joining Border Strips" on page 17, sew the 2¾"-wide outer border strips together end to end. Referring to "Straight-Sewn Borders with Corner Squares" on page 18, measure the quilt, trim, and sew the outer border strips to the quilt top, adding a 2¾" corner square to each end of the top and bottom borders.

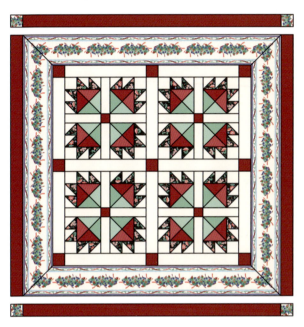

Finishing the Quilt

1. Layer the quilt top, batting, and backing; baste. Quilt as desired.

2. Trim the batting and backing even with the edges of the quilt top. Sew the binding to the edges of the quilt.

3. Make and attach a label to your finished quilt.

The Quilt That Refused to Be Gold

THE QUILT THAT REFUSED TO BE GOLD by Mary Hickey, Seattle, Washington, 1999.

Machine quilted by Frankie Schmitt.

Sometimes I start out making a quilt that I have planned carefully and wind up making something else entirely. When I started this quilt, I thought I would like to make a quilt in fall colors, something very simple, with a lot of rusts, golds, and browns—maybe sage green and a few peaches—but, definitely golds and rusts. I started by making some brown stars with sage green corners. The project seemed to be going smoothly. I prepared to search through the golds, but the box of gold fabric seemed to have been misplaced. Then, the red fabrics kept sneaking into the rust stars, and the rust fabrics refused to move out of their boxes. Finally a rosy floral, lurking on a shelf above the sewing machine, pretended to fall onto the table next to the blocks. I gave up and allowed the fabrics to choose themselves for the quilt.

However, this was not quite the end of my stumbling and bumbling. Fortunately I have an electric seam ripper (see page 10 for more about the electric seam ripper), because the peach fabric that looked so pretty when I auditioned it on my design wall, looked ghastly after I had sewn the top together. Out went the peach, in came the dainty floral with no peaches, golds, or browns. I really enjoyed making the quarter-square triangle units, so I decided to make more and add a pieced border. By then, I was pretty flustered, so I quickly sewed the pieced border and the rosy floral border to the quilt top and quit. —MH

FINISHED QUILT SIZE: 47" x 47"
FINISHED BLOCK SIZE: 7½"

Star block

Materials 42"-wide fabric

* ⅝ yd. muslin for star background
* ½ yd. light green check for background in pieced border

* ½ yd. pink floral print for background in pieced border
* ⅝ yd. dark brown print for stars and pieced border
* ½ yd. medium brown print for centers of stars and pieced border
* ½ yd. dark red print for stars and pieced border
* ½ yd. medium red print for centers of stars and pieced border
* ¼ yd. sage green print for corners of brown stars
* ¼ yd. small-scale floral print for corners of red stars
* 1 yd. large-scale floral print for plain squares and setting triangles
* ¾ yd. rosy floral print for outer border
* 2⅞ yds. for backing
* 50" x 50" piece of batting
* ⅝ yd. for binding

Cutting

ALL MEASUREMENTS include ¼"-wide seam allowances.

From the muslin, cut:
- 2 squares, 18" x 18", for quarter-square triangle units in stars

From the light green check, cut:
- 2 squares, 15" x 15", for quarter-square triangle units in border

From the pink floral print, cut:
- 2 squares, 15" x 15", for quarter-square triangle units in border

From the dark brown print, cut:
- 1 square, 18" x 18", for quarter-square triangle units in stars
- 1 square, 15" x 15", for quarter-square triangle units in border

From the medium brown print, cut:
- 1 square, 15" x 15", for quarter-square triangle units in border
- 5 squares, 3" x 3", for centers of brown stars

From the dark red print, cut:
- 1 square, 15" x 15", for quarter-square triangle units in border
- 1 square, 18" x 18", for quarter-square triangle units in stars

From the medium red print, cut:
- 1 square, 15" x 15", for quarter-square triangle units in border
- 4 squares, 3" x 3", for centers of red stars

From the sage green print, cut:
- 2 strips, 3" x 42"; crosscut strips into 20 squares, 3" x 3", for corners of brown stars

From the small-scale floral print, cut:
- 2 strips, 3" x 42"; crosscut strips into 16 squares, 3" x 3", for corners of red stars

From the large-scale floral print, cut:
- 4 squares, 8" x 8", for plain squares
- 2 squares, 13½" x 13½"; cut squares twice diagonally to make 8 side setting triangles
- 2 squares, 7" x 7"; cut squares once diagonally to make 4 corner setting triangles

From the rosy floral print, cut:
- 5 strips, 4¾" x 42", for outer border

Making the Blocks

1. Referring to "Making Quarter-Square Triangle Units" on page 14, pair an 18" muslin and dark brown square to make 20 half-square triangle units as follows:

   Cut the strips 3⅜" wide.
   Cut the segments 3⅜" wide.
   Cut the squares 3⅜" x 3⅜".

   Cut the squares in half, perpendicular to the seam line, to make 40 half units.

Make 20.

2. Assemble the muslin and brown half units as shown to make quarter-square triangle units. Make 20 units.

Make 20.

3. Repeat step 1 with an 18" muslin and dark red square to make 16 half-square triangle units. Cut the units in half, perpendicular to the seam line, to make 32 half units. Assemble the muslin and red half units to make quarter-square triangle units. Make 16 units.

Make 16.

4. Assemble the quarter-square triangle units and 3" squares as shown to make a Star block. Make 5 brown stars and 4 red stars.

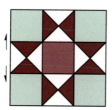

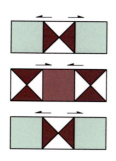

Make 5.

Make 4.

Making the Pieced Border

1. Referring to "Making Quarter-Square Triangle Units" on page 14, pair the following 15" squares:

> light green check and dark brown
> light green check and medium brown
> pink floral and dark red
> pink floral and medium red

Cut the strips 3⅜" wide.
Cut the segments 3⅜" wide.
Cut the squares 3⅜" x 3⅜".

Cut 13 half-square triangle units from each color combination (52 total). Cut the units in half, perpendicular to the seam, to make 26 half units of each color combination (104 total). Join the half units as shown to make 24 brown/green quarter-square triangle units and 24 red/floral quarter-square triangle units.

Make 24.

Make 24.

2. Sew the remaining 4 red half units together as shown to make the corner unit. Make 2 units. Repeat with the remaining 4 brown half units. Make 2 units.

Make 2.

Make 2.

3. Sew 12 triangle units together as shown to make each of 4 borders. Sew a corner unit to each end of 2 of the borders, making sure to orient them correctly.

Make 2 side borders.

Make 1 bottom border.

Make 1 top border.

Assembling the Quilt Top

1. Referring to the diagram below, arrange the blocks and corner and side setting triangles in 5 diagonal rows.

2. Referring to "Making Diagonal-Set Quilts" on pages 15–16, pin and sew the blocks together in diagonal rows. Carefully pin and sew the rows together, matching the seams. Use a long ruler to trim the edges of the quilt ¼" from the block points.

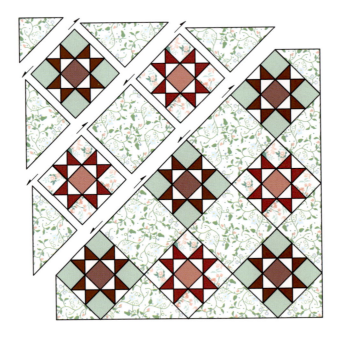

3. Sew a pieced side border to opposite sides of the quilt top. Press the seams toward the center of the quilt top. Sew the remaining pieced borders to the top and bottom edges.

4. Referring to "Joining Border Strips" on page 17, sew the 4¾"-wide outer border strips together end to end as needed. Referring to "Straight-Sewn Borders" on page 17, measure the quilt, trim, and sew the outer border strips to the quilt top. Press the seams toward the outer border.

Finishing the Quilt

1. Layer the quilt top, batting, and backing; baste. Quilt as desired.

2. Trim the batting and backing even with the edges of the quilt top. Sew the binding to the edges of the quilt.

3. Make and attach a label to your finished quilt.

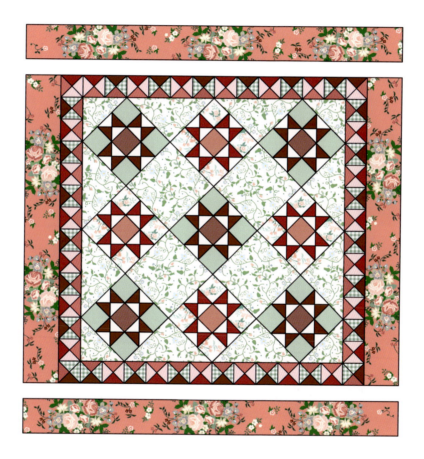

Template Quilts

Tilted Pinwheels

TILTED PINWHEELS by Joan Hanson, Seattle, Washington, 1997.

The Pinwheel block is another old favorite that we have updated by adding long, skinny corner triangles around each pinwheel. By alternating the blocks with medium and dark corners, a secondary pinwheel design emerges. If you have trouble seeing this, try squinting your eyes, looking through a reducing glass, or if you are like us, removing your glasses. I used scraps of our four favorite colors—red, blue, yellow, and green—for the pinwheels, but almost any color combination would work, as long as you stick with the contrast of the medium and dark colors.

This quilt represents an interesting variation on the quarter-square triangle. Instead of cutting and sewing the quarter-square triangles the way we did in the previous quilts, we used templates to cut the pieces for this block. Once you get the pieces all cut out and arranged, you'll find that these blocks go together easily and quickly. —JH

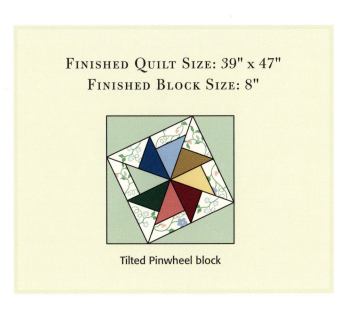

FINISHED QUILT SIZE: 39" x 47"
FINISHED BLOCK SIZE: 8"

Tilted Pinwheel block

Materials 42"-wide fabric

* ⅝ yd. light print for background
* 1 yd. *total* of 3 medium red, 3 medium blue, 3 medium yellow, and 3 medium green scraps
* 1 yd. *total* of 3 dark red, 3 dark blue, 3 dark yellow, and 3 dark green scraps
* ½ yd. light floral print for inner border
* ⅔ yd. dark blue print for outer border
* 1½ yds. for backing
* 42" x 50" piece of batting
* ½ yd. for binding

Cutting

ALL MEASUREMENTS include ¼"-wide seam allowances. Make plastic or cardboard templates from the patterns on page 143. Be sure to mark the template letter and grain line on each template.

From the light print, cut:
* 2 strips, 4¼" x 42", crosscut into 12 squares, 4¼" x 4¼"; cut squares twice diagonally to make 48 triangles
* 5 strips, 1⅜" x 42"; cut 48 of template A from the strips

NOTE: *Pattern A is an asymmetrical shape; cut the template with right side of fabric facing up.*

From each of the medium reds, medium blues, medium yellows, and medium greens, cut:
* 1 square, 4¼" x 4¼" (12 squares total); cut squares twice diagonally to make 48 triangles

From each of 6 medium colors, cut:
* 4 of template B (24 total)

NOTE: *Pattern B is an asymmetrical shape; cut the template with right side of fabric facing up.*

From each of the dark reds, dark blues, dark yellows, and dark greens, cut:
* 1 square, 4¼" x 4¼" (12 total); cut squares twice diagonally to make 48 triangles

From each of 6 dark colors, cut:

- 4 of template B (24 total)

NOTE: *Pattern B is an asymmetrical shape; cut the template with right side of fabric facing up.*

From the light floral print, cut:

- 4 strips, 3" x 42", for inner border

From the dark blue print, cut:

- 4 strips, 5¼" x 42", for outer border

From 1 of the dark red prints, cut:

- 4 squares, 5¼" x 5¼", for corner squares in outer border

Making the Blocks

1. Arrange the pinwheel triangles as shown, alternating the medium and dark colors in a way that is pleasing to you. In our quilt, we paired a medium and dark of the same color next to each other, but you can try another arrangement. The only rule is to alternate a medium color and a dark color so your pinwheel looks like it is spinning.

2. Place the background pieces around your pinwheel to complete the center of the block as shown. Sew a background piece to the pinwheel piece next to it.

3. Sew the diagonal seams as shown. Sew 2 sections together to make half of a block. Repeat to make the other half. Sew the 2 halves together. Press the seam open to distribute the bulk.

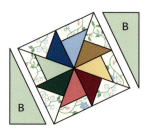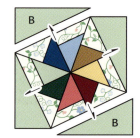

Make 12.

4. Sew 2 matching B pieces to opposite sides of a pinwheel. Be sure you are placing the long side (the "bias" edge) of piece B next to the pinwheel. Sew 2 B pieces of the same color to the remaining sides of the pinwheel. Make 6 blocks with medium corners and 6 blocks with dark corners.

Make 6 with medium corners.

Make 6 with dark corners.

Assembling the Quilt Top

1. Referring to the diagram below, arrange the blocks in 4 horizontal rows of 3 blocks each, alternating the blocks with the dark and medium corners. This forms a secondary pinwheel design where the blocks meet.

2. Referring to "Making Straight-Set Quilts" on page 15, pin and sew the blocks together in horizontal rows. Carefully pin and sew the rows together, matching the seams.

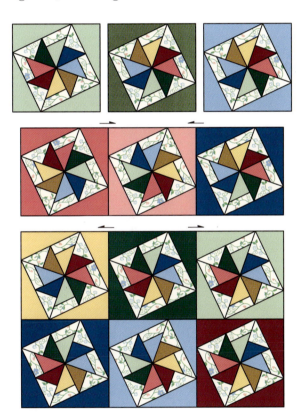

3. Referring to "Borders with Mitered Corners" on pages 18–19, measure the quilt, trim, and sew the 3"-wide inner border strips to the quilt top. Miter the corners.

4. Referring to "Straight-Sewn Borders with Corner Squares" on page 18, measure the quilt, trim, and sew the 5¼"-wide outer border strips to the quilt top, adding a 5¼" corner square to each end of the top and bottom borders.

Finishing the Quilt

1. Layer the quilt top, batting, and backing; baste. Quilt as desired.

2. Trim the batting and backing even with the edges of the quilt top. Sew the binding to the edges of the quilt.

3. Make and attach a label to your finished quilt.

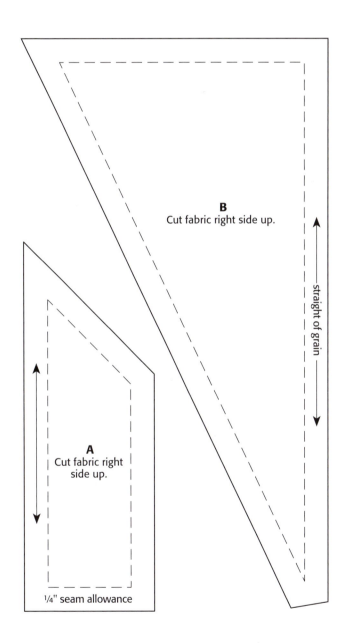

B
Cut fabric right side up.

straight of grain

A
Cut fabric right side up.

¼" seam allowance

Hearts and Arrows

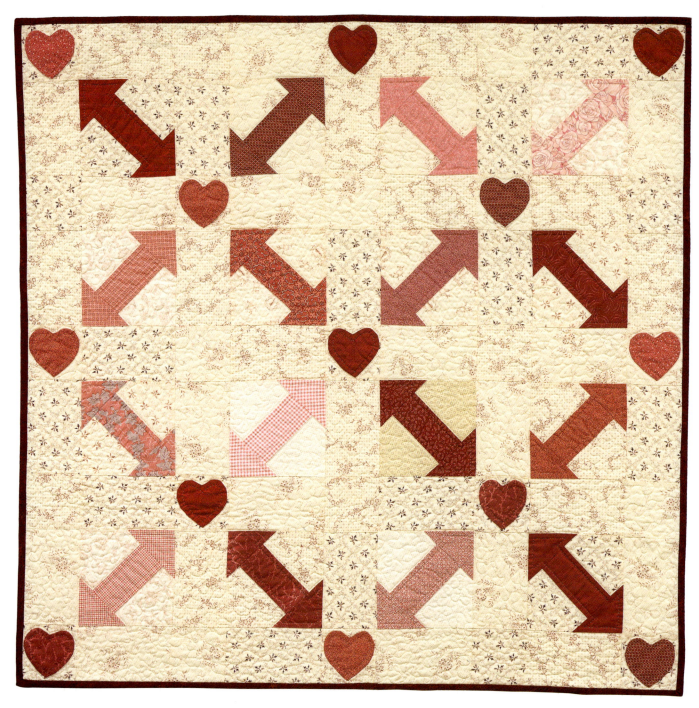

HEARTS AND ARROWS by Joan Hanson, Seattle, Washington, 1998.

For many years, Mary and I have been members of the Monday Night Bowling League. When our quilt group was looking for a name, we decided that we would be a bowling group that didn't bowl (although there is a bowling ball that mysteriously travels from one member's home to another). Most of the time we are each very involved with projects of our own that we enjoy sharing with the group. Once in a while, we decide to do a group project. Several years ago, we decided to make blocks that a member would win. The more blocks you made, the better your chances of winning. The Arrow blocks in this delightful quilt were ones that I was lucky enough to win. This is a very easy block and one that works well for a friendship signature block. Since Marsha McCloskey is a fellow "bowler," we used her Staples fabrics for the background prints, and assorted pinks and reds for the arrows. Set with wide sashing and a few hearts for the arrows to aim at, this project finishes in a jiffy. —JH

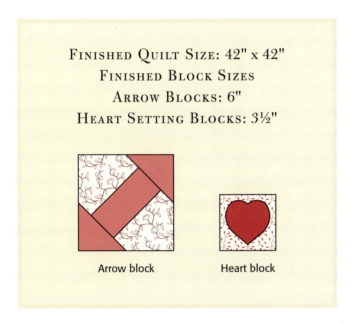

FINISHED QUILT SIZE: 42" x 42"
FINISHED BLOCK SIZES
ARROW BLOCKS: 6"
HEART SETTING BLOCKS: 3½"

Arrow block   Heart block

Materials 42"-wide fabric

* 1¾ yds. *total* assorted light prints for background
* ¾ yd. *total* assorted pinks and reds for hearts and arrows
* 2⅝ yds. for backing
* 46" x 46" piece of batting
* ½ yd. for binding

Cutting

ALL MEASUREMENTS include ¼"-wide seam allowances.

From the assorted light prints, cut a total of:
* 16 squares, 5½" x 5½"; crosscut squares once diagonally to make 32 triangles
* 40 strips, 4" x 6½", for sashing
* 25 squares, 4" x 4", for sashing squares

From the assorted pinks and reds, cut a total of:
* 16 rectangles, 2½" x 4¾", for arrows
* 16 squares, 3⅞" x 3⅞"; crosscut squares once diagonally to make 32 triangles for arrow points
* 26 squares, 4¼" x 4¼", for hearts

Making the Arrow Blocks

1. Make a plastic or cardboard template of pattern A. Use the template to trim the corners of the light print triangles as shown. Make 32.

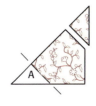

5½"   Make 32.

2. Sew a light print piece made in step 1 to opposite sides of a 2½" x 4¾" pink or red rectangle (arrow) as shown. Make 16.

Make 16.

3. Using matching fabrics, sew a red or pink triangle (arrow point) to each end of a unit from step 2 as shown. Make 16 blocks.

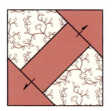

Make 16.

Making the Heart Blocks

1. Prepare the hearts for appliqué, referring to "Making the Hearts: Face-and-Turn Appliqué" on page 25. Use the 4¼" squares of pink or red and pattern B on page 147.

2. Appliqué a heart in the center of 13 of the light print sashing squares.

Make 13.

Assembling the Quilt Top

1. Referring to the diagram below, arrange the blocks and sashing strips in 4 horizontal rows of 4 blocks and 5 sashing strips each. Alternate with 5 rows of 5 sashing squares and 4 sashing strips. Be sure that the arrows are all pointing at the hearts.

2. Referring to "Making Straight-Set Quilts" on page 15, pin and sew the units in horizontal rows. Carefully pin and sew the rows together, matching the seams.

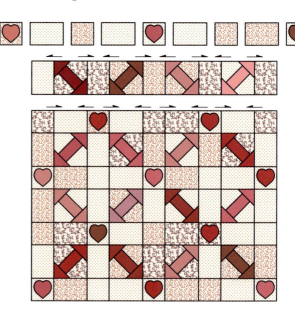

Finishing the Quilt

1. Layer the quilt top, batting, and backing; baste. Quilt as desired.

2. Trim the batting and backing even with the edges of the quilt top. Sew the binding to the edges of the quilt.

3. Make and attach a label to your finished quilt.

Quilting detail

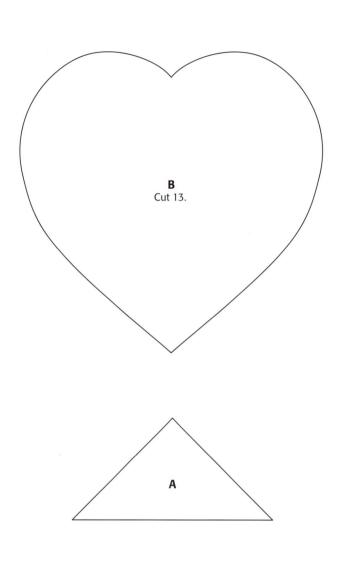

B
Cut 13.

A

Tillie's Posy Pots

TILLIE'S POSY POTS by Joan Hanson, Seattle, Washington, 1999.

Every morning, after getting everyone out the door to start their day, I go out for a long walk. Along my route, there are many charming older homes that I "supervise" as they are being remodeled and lovingly cared for. The simple little flowerpot block in this quilt was inspired by the shutter design on one of the houses that I pass by each day. The stem and flowerpot were machine appliquéd using black thread and a blanket stitch. The flowers are yo-yos with black button centers. All the fabrics are reproduction 1930s fabrics, using only reds, blues, greens, yellows, and blacks (no pinks or purples). The Chimney Stone block gives a wonderful diagonal frame to the flowerpot blocks and a pleasant rhythm to the quilt.

Matilda Everett, my grandmother, was an accomplished seamstress as well as an expert fisher-woman and crab catcher. My grandparents both loved to fish, and in the early 1940s, they purchased a beach cabin on Whidbey Island in Puget Sound. In the summers, Tillie would often ask, "Who wants fish for breakfast?" Then in the predawn hours, she would get up, put her fishing clothes on over her nightgown and go out fishing. She would row an old wooden skiff until she caught our breakfast. My grandfather was very proud of her and often boasted that, of the two of them, she always caught the biggest fish. I have named this quilt in her honor, for raising a family during the Depression and using her sewing skills to make something out of nothing to keep her family clothed. I was her first granddaughter and she delighted in making me dresses and my dolls dresses to match. As the mother of two boys, I hope someday to have granddaughters of my own to carry on the fishing and sewing traditions. —JH

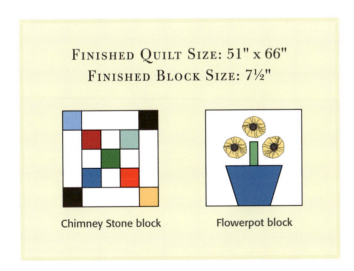

FINISHED QUILT SIZE: 51" x 66"
FINISHED BLOCK SIZE: 7½"

Chimney Stone block   Flowerpot block

Materials 42"-wide fabric

* 2 yds. background print for blocks and middle border
* 2½ yds. *total* of assorted 1930s fabrics for blocks and inner border
* ¾ yds. red plaid for outer border
* 2½ yds. for backing
* 53" x 68" piece of batting
* ½ yd. for binding
* 51 buttons for yo-yo centers
* Black embroidery thread

Cutting

ALL MEASUREMENTS include ¼"-wide seam allowances.

From the background print, cut:

- 17 squares, 8" x 8", for appliqué blocks
- 4 strips, 2" x 42", for pieced blocks
- 2 strips, 5" x 42", for pieced blocks
- 2 strips, 5" x 42"; crosscut strips into 36 rectangles, 2" x 5", for pieced blocks
- 5 strips, 1¼" x 42", for middle border

From the assorted 1930s fabrics, cut a total of:

- 14 strips, 2" x 42"; crosscut 8 to 9 squares from each strip for a total of 124 squares, 2" x 2", for the inner border. Use the remainder of the strips for the pieced blocks.

From the red plaid, cut:

- 5 strips, 4¾" x 42", for outer border

Making the Chimney Stone Blocks

1. Arrange an assortment of 2"-wide 1930s print strips in different lengths on either side of a 2"-wide background strip as shown. Sew the short strips together end to end to make one long strip approximately 42" long. The shorter the strips, the scrappier your quilt will be. Sew the long strips together to make a strip set. Make 2 strip sets. Crosscut the strip sets into 36 segments, 2" wide.

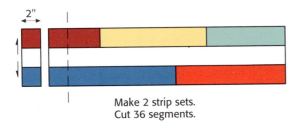

Make 2 strip sets.
Cut 36 segments.

2. Arrange an assortment of 2"-wide 1930s print strips between two 2"-wide background strips as shown. Short strips will give a scrappier look. Sew the short strips together, then join the long strips to make 1 strip set. Crosscut the strip set into 18 segments, 2" wide.

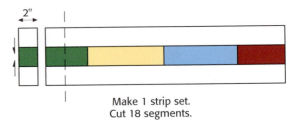

Make 1 strip set.
Cut 18 segments.

3. Join 2 segments from step 1 and 1 segment from step 2 as shown to make a nine-patch unit. Make 18 units.

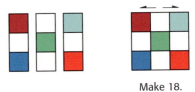

Make 18.

4. Arrange an assortment of 2"-wide 1930s print strips on either side of a 5"-wide background strip as shown. Sew the short strips together, then join the long strips to make a strip set. Make 2 strip sets. Crosscut the strip sets into 36 segments, 2" wide.

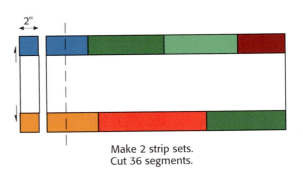

Make 2 strip sets.
Cut 36 segments.

5. Add the 2" x 5" background rectangles to the top and bottom of the nine-patch units. Sew the segments made in step 4 to the opposite sides of the nine-patch units to make a Chimney Stone block. Make 18 blocks.

Make 18.

Making the Flowerpot Blocks

USE THE patterns on pages 152 and 153.

1. Make plastic or cardboard templates of the flowerpot and stem patterns. Trace around the flowerpot template and cut 17 from the 1930s prints, adding a scant ¼" seam allowance around the traced line as you cut. Repeat for the stems, using green 1930s prints.

2. Fold the edges under ¼" on each of the stems and flowerpots as shown. You do not need to turn under the edges on the bottom of the stem or the flowerpot.

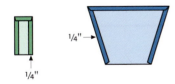

3. Position and pin a stem and a flowerpot on an 8" background square. Appliqué in place by hand or machine. Place the flowerpot so it covers the bottom raw edge of the stem.

Make 17.

4. Referring to "Making Yo-Yos" on page 153, make 3 matching circles for each flowerpot. Make a total of 51 circles.

NOTE: *The yo-yos will be added after the quilt is quilted so that they won't be in the way while you are quilting. When my husband, Jim, saw this quilt before the yo-yos were added, he asked if it was a lampshade quilt.*

Assembling the Quilt Top

1. Referring to the diagram below, arrange the blocks in 7 horizontal rows of 5 blocks each.

2. Referring to "Making Straight-Set Quilts" on page 15, pin and sew the blocks together in horizontal rows. Carefully pin and sew the rows together, matching the seams.

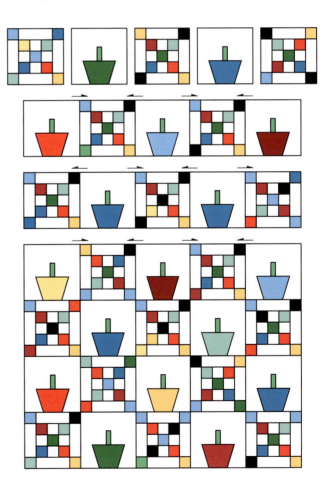

3. Using the 2" squares of 1930s prints, sew 35 squares together to make each of the side borders. Sew 27 squares together to make each of the top and bottom borders.

Make 2 side borders.

Make a top and a bottom border.

4. Sew a pieced side border to opposite sides of the quilt. Sew the remaining pieced borders to the top and bottom edges.

5. Referring to "Straight-Sewn Borders" on page 17, measure the quilt, trim, and sew the 1¼"-wide middle border strips to the quilt top. Repeat with the 4¾"-wide outer border strips.

Finishing the Quilt

1. Layer the quilt top, batting, and backing; baste. Quilt as desired.

2. Position the yo-yos as marked on the flowerpot blocks. Attach them, using a button and embroidery thread. Sew around the edge of the yo-yos with a running stitch and matching thread.

3. Trim the batting and backing even with the edges of the quilt top. Sew the binding to the quilt.

4. Make and attach a label to your finished quilt.

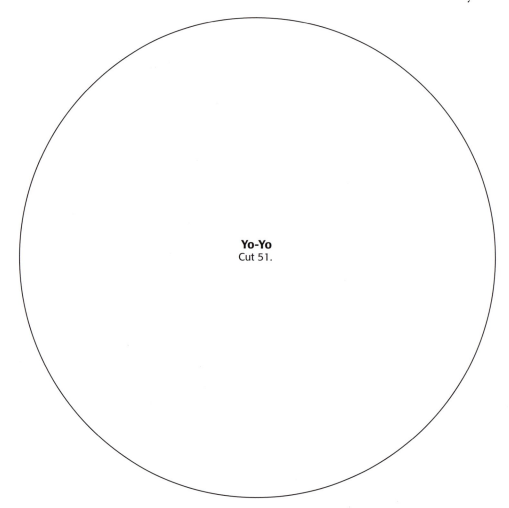

Yo-Yo
Cut 51.

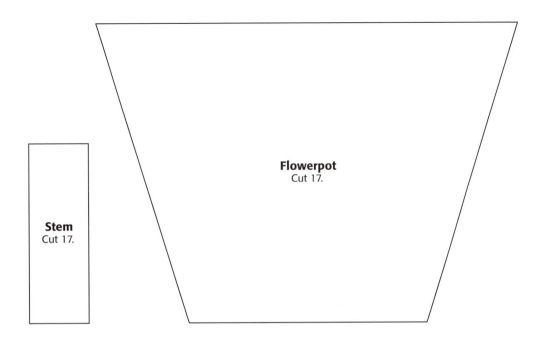

Flowerpot
Cut 17.

Stem
Cut 17.

Making Yo-Yos

1. Use the circle pattern on page 152 to cut a circle from a 1930s print. Do not add a seam allowance when cutting.

2. Turn under the edge of the circle a scant ¼" and sew around the edge, using a double thread of a matching color and a long running stitch.

3. Draw up the thread as tightly as possible and secure the thread by stitching several times in the same spot. Flatten into a yo-yo shape.

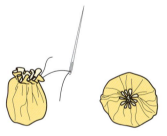

4. Secure the yo-yo to your block by stitching a button in the middle and by sewing a running stitch in matching thread around the outer edge. It's a good idea to wait until after your project is quilted to apply the yo-yos so that they won't be pinched in your quilting frame or get stuck under your presser foot.

Finishing the Quilt

IF YOU ARE reading this part of *The Simple Joys of Quilting*, you have probably made a quilt top and are ready to quilt it. What a spectacular accomplishment! Congratulations!

A quilt has three layers: the top, the batting, and the backing. The batting is the fluffy layer in the middle of the quilt. Before a quilt can be quilted, you must baste the layers together. However, depending on the type of quilting you intend to do, you may want to mark the quilting lines on the quilt top before basting the layers together.

The stitching that holds the layers together and forms the sculpted designs is called quilting, and it is from these stitches that quilts get their name. The quilting stitches are often simple outlines of the patches, although quiltmakers frequently add generous echoes of the shapes and elaborate patterns that add a completely new dimension of design to the surface. As you plan your quilting designs, keep in mind that the layers of fabric in a seam allowance are difficult to hand quilt, so plan your design to avoid stitching across too many seams.

Marking the Quilting Lines

CAREFULLY PRESS the quilt top and trace the quilting designs onto it. Many quilters draw the design lightly with a mechanical pencil. Powdered chalk dispensers, white pencils, and slivers of soap are all useful for marking quilting lines on dark fabrics. Test your marking tool on a fabric scrap to be sure the marks can be removed easily.

If you mark the quilting design before you baste, you can trace your design onto all but the darkest fabrics. You will need a light source behind the design. Tape the design to a window and tape your quilt over it, or make a temporary light table by supporting a piece of glass or Plexiglas over a small lamp. For dark fabrics, you may need to use a stencil and draw on your quilting design with chalk, soap, or a white pencil.

Making a Backing

CUT A quilt backing that is at least 2" larger than your quilt top all around. For example, if your quilt top is 36" x 36", you will need a piece of backing that is 40" x 40". If your quilt is larger than the standard width of fabric, you will have to stitch two or more pieces of fabric together to make the backing. Trim away the selvages before sewing the lengths together. Press the seams open to make quilting the top easier.

Many quilters enjoy piecing the large scraps left over from the quilt top into the back of the quilt. This is an area in which you can be very free and whimsical.

Choosing the Batting

BATTING COMES packaged in standard bed sizes and by the yard. A thin batting usually makes quilting easier. Cut the batting at least 2" larger than your quilt top all around.

Layering and Basting

SPREAD THE backing, wrong side up, on a clean, flat surface. Use masking tape to anchor the backing to the surface without stretching the fabric. Spread the quilt batting on the backing, making sure it covers the entire backing and is smooth. Center the pressed and marked top on the batting and backing, right side up. Align the borders and straight lines of the quilt top with the edges of the backing. Pin the quilt's layers together along the edge with large straight pins.

BASTING FOR HAND QUILTING

Hand baste the three layers together, using a long needle and light-colored thread. If you thread your needle without cutting the thread off the spool, you will be able to baste at least one or two rows without rethreading your needle. Starting at the center of the quilt, use large running stitches to baste across the quilt from side to side and top to bottom. Continue basting, creating a grid of parallel lines 6" to 8" apart. Complete the basting with a line of careful stitches around the outside edges. This will keep the edges from raveling while you quilt and will also keep them aligned when you stitch the binding to the quilt.

After basting is complete, remove the pins and masking tape.

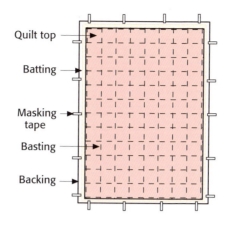

BASTING FOR MACHINE QUILTING

Although stapling systems and adhesive basting sprays are available, most machine quilters use 1" safety pins to baste a quilt. Safety pins are easy to remove when an area has been quilted. Start pinning in the center and work toward the outer edges of the quilt, spacing the pins 4" to 6" apart. Insert the pin as you would a straight pin. Avoid pinning over seam lines where you intend to stitch in-the-ditch and avoid pinning over your design lines. Use a needle and thread to baste a line of stitches around the outside edges.

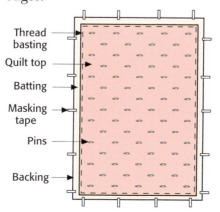

Remove the quilt from the hard surface and close the safety pins.

Hand Quilting

FOR SOME quilters, the best part of the process of making a quilt is the hand quilting. It is relaxing to sit and stitch while visiting with friends or riding in the car. Quilting is simply a short running stitch that goes through all three layers of the quilt. Hand quilt in a frame, in a hoop, on a tabletop, or on your lap. Use a heavy thread designed for hand quilting. The thicker thread is less likely to tangle than regular sewing thread. Use a short sturdy needle (called a Between) in a size 7. Use a thimble with a rim around the top edge to help push the needle through the layers.

1. Cut the thread 24" long and tie a small knot. Starting about 1" from where you want the quilting to begin, insert the needle through the top and batting only. Bring the needle up where the quilting will start. Gently tug on the knot until it pops through the quilt top and catches in the batting.

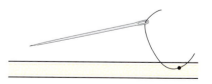

Gently pop knot into batting.

2. Insert the needle and push it straight down through all the layers. Then rock the needle up and down through all layers, "loading" three or four stitches on the needle. Push the needle with a thimble on your middle finger; then pull the needle through, aiming toward yourself as you work. Place your other hand under the quilt to make sure the needle has penetrated all three layers with each stitch. Continue in this way, taking small, even stitches through all three layers.

3. To end a line of quilting, make a small knot close to the quilt top and then take one stitch through the top and batting only. Pop the knot through the fabric into the batting. Clip the thread near the surface of the quilt.

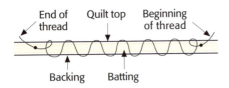

End of thread   *Quilt top*   *Beginning of thread*

Backing   *Batting*

Machine Quilting

As QUILTERS find that they are able to piece more quilt tops than they can quilt by hand, they realize that machine quilting is a practical alternative to hand quilting. In the last few years, machine quilting has become a beautiful art form in its own right. Machine quilting has become so important to quiltmakers that we will take some extra time and space to give you a thorough introduction to it.

Choose a small quilt for your first machine-quilting project because it will be easier to guide through your sewing machine. Plan a quilting design that involves continuous long straight lines and gentle curves.

Use either a fine 100% cotton silk-finish thread or a very fine, high-quality .004m nylon thread made specifically for machine quilting for the top thread in your machine. Nylon thread comes in clear for lighter fabrics and a smoke color for darker fabrics. Thread your bobbin with the fine 100% cotton thread.

A walking or even-feed foot moves the top layer of fabric through your machine at the same speed as the bottom layer. Moving the quilt layers evenly through the machine keeps the quilt from puckering. Use this type of foot for straight-line, grid quilting and large, simple curves.

Walking foot

Use a darning foot for curved designs and stipple quilting. This allows free fabric movement under the foot of your sewing machine. This is called free-motion quilting and, with practice, you can produce beautiful quilting designs quickly.

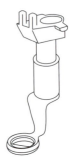

Darning foot

Choose designs that have continuous lines and that don't require a lot of starting and stopping. Lower the feed dogs on your machine when quilting with a darning foot. This allows you to guide the fabric under the needle as if the needle were a stationary pencil. The stitch length is determined by the speed with which you run the machine and how much you move the fabric under the needle. You will get used to it with a little practice. The effort is well worth it, as you can practically complete a quilt before the seventh-inning stretch.

Practice first with layers of fabrics and scrap batting until you get the feel of controlling the motion of the fabric with your hands. Running the machine fairly fast enables you to sew smoother lines of quilting. If you have a "needle down" feature on your machine, it is useful for all machine quilting. To start and stop, tie off your thread by shortening the stitch length for the first and last ⅛" to ¼". Stitch some scribbles, zigzags, and curves. Try a heart or a star. Make sure to adjust your chair to a comfortable height.

Roll your layered quilt up like a scroll. Starting in the center and using the walking foot, stitch all the lines in one direction. Always start at the same end so that the rows won't pull in opposite directions. Reroll your quilt in the other direction and repeat stitching the straight lines in that direction. Next repeat with the diagonal lines. Remove the pins as you get the areas secured. Now take a break and stretch your back.

When you have completed all the straight-line quilting, switch to your darning foot, lower the feed dogs, and start the free-motion quilting. Stipple quilting in the background areas gives a lovely texture and doesn't require any prior marking. Pretend that you are drawing jigsaw-puzzle lines (lots of curvy lines without any loops) on your quilt. Try to end up

at an intersection where you can "jump" across to the next area to be stitched. When all the quilting is completed, remove any stray pins, but leave the basting stitches around the edges. Trim the batting and backing even with the quilt top. Make sure the corners are square. What a wonderful moment this is!

Free-motion quilting

Making a Sleeve

1. If you are going to hang your quilt, attach a sleeve or rod pocket to the back before you bind the quilt. From the left-over backing fabric, cut a piece the width of your quilt by 8". On each end, fold over a ½" hem and then fold under again another ½".

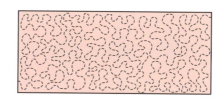
½" ½"

2. Fold the strip in half the long way, right sides together, and machine baste the raw edges to the top edge of your quilt. Your quilt should be about an inch wider on both sides. Slipstitch the bottom edge of

the sleeve edge to the backing fabric.

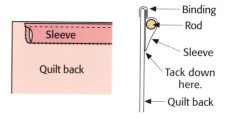
Binding
Rod
Sleeve
Tack down here.
Quilt back

Binding the Quilt

BINDING STRIPS are usually cut on the bias grain of the fabric because they wear better and look smoother than straight-grain strips. If you have a striped fabric or other fabric with a directional design, cutting on the straight grain may give you the look you want.

1. To make bias-binding strips, use the 45°-angle line on your large cutting ruler as a guide to cut enough strips to go around the perimeter of the quilt, plus a few extra inches for joining the strips and turning corners. Cut the strips 2" wide.

2. Join the strips together with ¼" diagonal seams. Press the seams open.

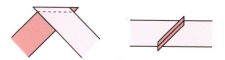

3. Feed your long 2"-wide bias strips through a 1" bias-tape maker (a great little gadget available at your quilt shop).

Press with a steam iron as you pull the bias-tape maker along. Two folds will magically appear in your fabric, giving you a bias tape that is 1" wide with ½" folded under on each edge.

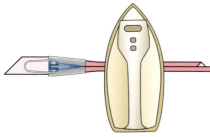

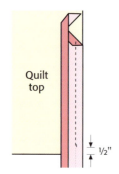

Edges just meet on wrong side.

4. Open up one edge of your strip and turn under the diagonal edge ½" to make a finished edge. Starting at the center bottom of your quilt and using the ½" fold line as a guide, stitch the binding to the quilt, smoothing it in place as you stitch. Stop your stitching ½" from the corner of the quilt and backstitch. Remove the quilt from the machine.

Quilt top

½"

5. Fold the binding at a 45° angle away from the quilt and then down so it is even with the next side. Start stitching at the edge, using the same seam allowance as before.

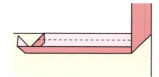

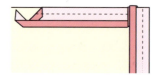

6. Continue stitching around all four sides, catching the sleeve on the top edge. When you get back to where you started, lap the end over the beginning and trim off the excess.

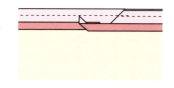

7. Fold the binding around to the back of the quilt and blind-stitch it down, using your machine-stitching line as a guide. A miter will form at each corner. Fold the corners in place and stitch.

Fold first.

Quilt back

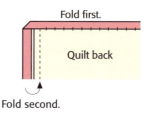

Fold second.

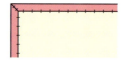

Adding a Quilt Label

LABELING YOUR quilt is an important finishing touch. Use a plain fabric that coordinates with your backing fabric for your label and include the name of the quilt, your name, your city and state, date, the recipient if it is a gift, and any other interesting or important information. This can be embroidered, cross-stitched, printed on your computer, or written with a permanent pen. If you are using a computer or a pen, iron freezer paper to the back of the fabric to stabilize the fabric.

About the Authors

ONGTIME FRIENDS AND quilting buddies, Joan Hanson and Mary Hickey have shared a friendship and profession for twenty years. They team up frequently to laugh, tell stories, play with colors and blocks, and call it work. Of course, the colors are fabric and the blocks are quilt blocks.

Joan and Mary are known for creating charming quilts and writing clear instructions. Each of these talented women has written numerous successful quilting books. In 1995, they decided to put their creative energies together and write a comprehensive book covering many quiltmaking techniques. The resulting book is the award-winning *The Joy of Quilting*.

The goal in the classes Joan and Mary teach and in the books they write has always been to introduce new quilters to simple techniques for making lovely quilts. More importantly, they want to communicate the joy that comes from making quilts and sharing them with friends and loved ones. *The Simple Joys of Quilting* continues that tradition. Its pages are filled with easy, beautiful quilts, gentle encouragement, and humorous stories.

In addition to quilting, these dear friends share a passion for collecting dishes and old furniture. They are both dedicated baseball fans and love to spend time enjoying the beaches of Puget Sound.

Mary Hickey, left, and Joan Hanson, right

new and bestselling titles from

Martingale™
& COMPANY
America's Best-Loved Craft & Hobby Books™

That Patchwork Place®

America's Best-Loved Quilt Books®

NEW RELEASES
Artful Album Quilts
Biblical Blocks
Christmas at That Patchwork Place™
Color Moves
Colorwash Bargello Quilts
Country Threads
Creating Quilts with Simple Shapes
Creating with Paint
The Decorated Porch
Easy Paper-Pieced Baby Quilts
Flannel Quilts
In the Studio with Judy Murrah
Instant Fabric
More Quick Watercolor Quilts
Paper Piece a Flower Garden
Patchwork Picnic
Scrap Frenzy

APPLIQUÉ
Artful Appliqué
Colonial Appliqué
Red and Green: An Appliqué Tradition
Rose Sampler Supreme
Your Family Heritage: Projects in Appliqué

BABY QUILTS
The Quilted Nursery
Quilts for Baby: Easy as ABC
More Quilts for Baby: Easy as ABC
Even More Quilts for Baby: Easy as ABC

HOLIDAY QUILTS
Easy and Fun Christmas Quilts
Paper Piece a Merry Christmas
A Snowman's Family Album Quilt
Welcome to the North Pole

LEARNING TO QUILT
Basic Quiltmaking Techniques for:
  Borders and Bindings
  Curved Piecing
  Divided Circles
  Eight-Pointed Stars
  Hand Appliqué
  Machine Appliqué
  Strip Piecing
The Joy of Quilting
The Quilter's Handbook
Your First Quilt Book (or it should be!)

PAPER PIECING
50 Fabulous Paper-Pieced Stars
A Quilter's Ark
Easy Machine Paper Piecing
Needles and Notions
Paper-Pieced Curves
Show Me How to Paper Piece

ROTARY CUTTING
101 Fabulous Rotary-Cut Quilts
365 Quilt Blocks a Year Perpetual Calendar
Fat Quarter Quilts
Lap Quilting Lives!
Quick Watercolor Quilts
Quilts from Aunt Amy
Spectacular Scraps
Time-Crunch Quilts

SMALL & MINIATURE QUILTS
Celebrate! with Little Quilts
Easy Paper-Pieced Miniatures
Little Quilts All Through the House

CRAFTS
300 Papermaking Recipes
The Art of Handmade Paper
  and Collage
The Art of Stenciling
Creepy Crafty Halloween
Gorgeous Paper Gifts
Grow Your Own Paper
Instant Fabric
Stamp with Style
Wedding Ribbonry

KNITTING
Comforts of Home
Fair Isle Sweaters Simplified
Knit It Your Way
Knitted Shawls, Stoles, and Scarves
Knitting with Novelty Yarns
Paintbox Knits
Simply Beautiful Sweaters
Simply Beautiful Sweaters for Men
Two Sticks and a String
The Ultimate Knitter's Guide
Welcome Home: Kaffe Fassett

Our books are available at bookstores and your favorite craft, fabric and yarn retailers. If you don't see the title you're looking for, visit us at www.martingale-pub.com or contact us at:

1-800-426-3126

International: 1-425-483-3313

Fax: 1-425-486-7596

E-mail: info@martingale-pub.com

For more information and a full list of our titles, visit our Web site or call for a free catalog.

Mission Statement

WE ARE *dedicated to providing quality products and service by working together to inspire creativity and to enrich the lives we touch.*